SPECIAL NEEDS IN ORDINARY SC
General Editor: Peter Mittler

UNIVERSITY OF
WOLVERHAMPTON

Special Needs in Ordinary Schools

General editor: Peter Mittler
Associate editors: James Hogg, Peter Pumfrey, Tessa Roberts,
Colin Robson
Honorary advisory board: Neville Bennett, Marion Blythman,
George Cooke, John Fish, Ken Jones, Sylvia Phillips, Klaus Wedell,
Phillip Williams

Titles in this series

Meeting Special Needs in Ordinary Schools:
An Overview

Seamus Hegarty

CASSELL

Cassell Educational Limited
Artillery House
Artillery Row
London SW1P 1RT

British Library Cataloguing in Publication Data

Hegarty, Seamus
    Meeting special needs in ordinary schools:
    an overview.—(Special needs in
    ordinary schools).
    1. Exceptional children—Education—
    Great Britain
    I. Title   II. Series
    371.9'0941   LC3986.G7

ISBN 0–304–31356–6

Typeset by Activity Ltd, Salisbury, Wilts
Printed and bound in Great Britain by
Biddles Ltd, Guildford and King's Lynn

First published 1987
Reprinted 1989

Last digit is print no: 9 8 7 6 5 4 3 2

Contents

Foreword: Towards education for all

AIMS

This series aims to support teachers as they respond to the challenge they face in meeting the needs of all children in their school, particularly those identified as having special educational needs.

Although there have been many useful publications in the field of special educational needs during the last decade, the distinguishing feature of the present series of volumes lies in their concern with specific areas of the curriculum in primary and secondary schools. We have tried to produce a series of conceptually coherent and professionally relevant books, each of which is concerned with ways in which children with varying levels of ability and motivation can be taught together. The books draw on the experience of practising teachers, teacher trainers and researchers and seek to provide practical guidelines on ways in which specific areas of the curriculum can be made more accessible to all children. The volumes provide many examples of curriculum adaptation, classroom activities, teacher–child interactions, as well as the mobilisation of resources inside and outside the school.

The volumes are organised largely in terms of age and subject groupings, but three 'overview' volumes have been prepared in order to provide an account of some major current issues and developments. Seamus Hegarty's *Meeting Special Needs in Ordinary Schools* gives an introduction to the field of special needs as a whole, whilst Sheila Wolfendale's *Primary Schools and Special Needs* and John Sayer's *Secondary Schools For All?* address issues more specifically concerned with primary and secondary schools respectively. We hope that curriculum specialists will find essential backgrounds and contextual material in these overview volumes.

In addition, a section of this series will be concerned with examples of obstacles to learning. All of these specific special needs can be seen on a continuum ranging from mild to severe, or from temporary and transient to long-standing or permanent. They include difficulties in learning or in adjustment and behaviour, as well as problems resulting largely from sensory or physical impairments or from difficulties of communication from whatever cause. We hope that teachers will consult the volumes in this section for guidance on working with children with specific difficulties.

The series aims to make a modest 'distance learning' contribution to meeting the needs of teachers working with the whole range of pupils with special educational needs by offering a set of resource materials relating to specific areas of the primary and secondary curriculum and by suggesting ways in which learning obstacles, whatever their origin, can be identified and addressed.

We hope that these materials will not only be used for private study but be subjected to critical scrutiny by school-based inservice groups sharing common curricular interests and by staff of institutions of higher education concerned with both special needs teaching and specific curriculum areas. The series has been planned to provide a resource for LEA advisers, specialist teachers from all sectors of the education service, educational psychologists, and teacher working parties. We hope that the books will provide a stimulus for dialogue and serve as catalysts for improved practice.

It is our hope that parents will also be encouraged to read about new ideas in teaching children with special needs so that they can be in a better position to work in partnership with teachers on the basis of an informed and critical understanding of current difficulties and developments. The goal of 'Education for All' can only be reached if we succeed in developing a working partnership between teachers, pupils, parents, and the community at large.

The publishers and I would like to thank the many people – too numerous to mention – who have helped to create this series. In particular we would like to thank the Associate Editors, James Hogg, Peter Pumfrey, Tessa Roberts and Colin Robson, for their active advice and guidance; the Honorary Advisory Board, Neville Bennett, Marion Blythman, George Cooke, John Fish, Ken Jones, Sylvia Phillips, Klaus Wedell and Phillip Williams, for their comments and suggestions; and the teachers, teacher trainers and special needs advisers who took part in our information surveys.

Professor Peter Mittler   University of Manchester
                                                        January 1987

Acknowledgements

My thanks are due to the many colleagues at the National Foundation for Educational Research whose thinking has stimulated mine. I am especially grateful to Jane Lever for her skilled secretarial support and to Peter Mittler for criticism which was both apt and constructive.

In memory of Donal

Introducing the characters

Peter is 11, good natured, and obliging but not very bright. He is slow to pick up new ideas and has great difficulty in remembering things. When left alone he often sits staring into space.

He lives with his mother and younger sister and has a close relationship with his grandmother. He does not know his father. Peter's mother did badly at school herself. She is more than content to leave responsibility for his schooling to the teachers, although she does not set much score by education or expect that it will do much for Peter. Their material circumstances are poor and Peter was often ill when he was younger.

Peter is now at the end of an undistinguished primary school career. He has been in a class with age peers throughout, but spent a great deal of time being taught in small groups of less able children. His academic progress has been limited, with reading and number skills several years below the average for his age. He applies himself willingly to any task set but quickly loses concentration. Cooking is the only activity he enjoys for its own sake. Efforts to build language and number work into practical cookery sessions have had limited success.

Peter is generally helpful and quite sociable, but does not have a particular friend at school. He expects to go on to secondary school with his classmates but does not really think about it.

Sheila is a 6-year-old with a sunny disposition who loves meeting people and makes friends wherever she goes. She is almost totally blind in one eye and has limited vision in the other. Her eyesight is deteriorating. She seems to be of average or above average intelligence.

Her parents were aware of her eyesight problems from early on and were determined that she would lead a full, normal life. They devour any scrap of information on visual impairment that they can find and are eager supporters of anything proposed by professionals. Sheila's infant teacher, who knew very little about visual impairment, felt that she was supporting Sheila's parents in educating her!

Sheila went to an ordinary play group with her mother in frequent attendance. She has been at the local primary school for two years now. So far, her academic progress has been limited. About once a month a teacher for the blind visits the school. Sheila's class teacher knows nothing about visual impairment apart from what she has picked up from the visiting teacher and Sheila's mother. Neither her parents nor the school are unduly worried as yet since the main target has been to settle her in. This has been very successful – Sheila is outgoing, popular, and eager to go to school. She is showing signs of having an unusual musical talent and has built up, by ear, a repertoire of simple tunes on the piano.

Her parents are keen for Sheila to stay in the ordinary school sector, and Sheila herself would be upset at having to move from her present school. They are concerned about the future, however. Sheila has had a succession of physical mishaps lately, possibly because of her deteriorating eyesight. Whilst they do not want to be over-protective they are afraid that she will lose her outgoing attitude and sense of adventure. They believe that the teaching she receives is inadequate. At the moment they can compensate by engaging in lots of language and other structured activities at home, but what will happen when the school curriculum becomes more demanding? They are aware too that the school does not have a music specialist.

John is 14, small for his age but physically very tough. In school he generally comes across as sullen and uncooperative. He can be aggressive and has been involved in several gang fights. Away from school and his mates he often feels inadequate and unsure of himself.

He comes from a Forces background. This has meant several moves and some prolonged absences on the part of his father. He has an older sister and a younger brother. Their behaviour is relatively normal and John is conscious of being something of a black sheep in the family. When his father is home he can be extremely strict and sometimes disciplines John harshly, though he is secretly proud of his toughness.

John attends a large comprehensive school. He does not like it any more than he liked any of his 4 previous schools. Most of the schools were glad to see the back of him as well. He is receiving virtually no formal education. His limited academic skills are anyway disguised by his disruptive behaviour. He tends to act up when presented with a challenge or any situation where he might be seen to fail. As a result, most of his teachers have given up making demands on him and have a tacit agreement that if he does not disrupt the lesson he will be left alone.

He is unpopular on account of his bullying and general unpleasantness, but is also something of a folk hero because of his rudeness to staff and the fact that he gets away with so much untoward behaviour. He is sexually precocious. Staff see him as disruptive and a thoroughly bad influence and will be glad when he leaves.

Juliet is a shy 12-year-old who always seems to be at the edge of whatever is going on. She is generally backward and has a slight speech defect. Outside home she avoids speaking as much as possible. She is the youngest of a large, close-knit family. Her brothers and sisters see 'poor Juliet' as the slow one of the family and are very protective of her. Her parents left Trinidad to settle in England some 30 years ago. Her father died 5 years ago.

Juliet goes to the local comprehensive school. She has spent the first year in mixed ability teaching groups, but will be streamed into slow learner sets for English and maths in the second year. Her teachers expect her to receive most of her education within the school's provision for slow learners. From time to time staff have queried whether she might not benefit from speech therapy but nothing has happened about it. She has few friends at school. She is slow in reaching puberty and this has added to her sense of isolation.

Colin is a 9-year-old who can be full of charm and good humour but is often very moody. He suffers from spina bifida and is generally confined to a wheelchair. Psychologists believe that he is above average in intelligence.

When Colin was born, and his condition diagnosed, his parents took it very hard. Their previous child had been still-born, and they decided not to have any more children. They have been dutiful and caring parents and have not stinted in their efforts for Colin, but have never managed to shake off a deep sense of the unfairness of life. Following several negative experiences with poorly briefed professionals, they tend to be demanding of services, including school, and do not hesitate to criticise.

Colin attends the local primary school, where some minor building alterations have been made to accommodate the special needs of some children. He is taught as part of a normal class. A classroom assistant helps with toileting during break-times. His class performance is average and all his teachers have been satisfied with his progress. His parents believe that he is not achieving his potential, however; they point to his undoubted verbal skills and the encouragement contained in psychologists' reports. Sometimes they wonder if he would not be more stretched academically in a special school.

Colin is not particularly popular in his class. He likes to have his own way and to have things done for him. He looks down on anybody who seems less intelligent than himself and is capable of being very sarcastic.

How are Peter, Sheila, John, Juliet, and Colin to be educated? Between them they pose a considerable challenge to the education system. They have the same right to education as other children and young people, but in practice they do not always obtain their rights. They are less likely than other children to receive an appropriate education that develops their academic potential to the full, and they are often cut off from age peers for the education that they do receive. Thus, in the examples above, education has virtually ceased for John, whilst the parents of both Sheila and Colin have specific worries about the future and how well the school is going to cope with their child's particular needs.

This is not a book about five individuals, but about the group they represent. Peter, Sheila, and the others have been introduced to remind us that education is about individuals, who are unique and may have very little in common. Abstract language and generic terms are sometimes necessary, but the underlying reality is one of individual children – who have only one chance at schooling. Their stories also serve to foreshadow some of the themes recurring throughout the book.

What of the broader group then? How can we characterise it? An initial description is to say that it is made up of all those who have difficulties of learning or adjustment at school. This may appear to be unhelpfully vague – and relative. It does not, for instance, say anything about the kind or degree of difficulty, nor where the difficulties come from, i.e. from the child or from the school or indeed from the interaction between the two.

The target group is discussed in more detail below, particularly in chapter 4, where the concept of special educational need is examined. We must be wary of using over-precise language. The group cannot be characterised accurately except by taking account of what is expected of children at school, and what individual schools do to help them achieve that. Whether or not a pupil is deemed to have difficulties at school depends on what sort of school provision is available to the pupil. There is wide variation in the nature and quality of provision on offer, and it can happen that a pupil's difficulties disappear, or are exacerbated, by a simple change of schools.

One way round all of this is to work on a numerical basis. We could agree that the 'bottom' five per cent, say, need extra attention. In fact, since the Warnock Report estimated in 1978 that approximately one in five pupils would require some special provision during their school careers, it has become increasingly common to speak of the 20 per cent of pupils who have special educational needs. This percentage is often subdivided into the 2 per cent who have traditionally attended special schools and the 18 per cent who have school difficulties of various kinds but attend ordinary schools. This is a crude way of looking at the group but it can be useful so long as it is remembered that the figures are rough estimates and conceal large differences between schools. It is also limited in that it is based on arbitrary cut-off points: there is nothing absolute about the 20 per cent or the 2 per cent figures. They are pragmatic estimates of the amount of school failure that calls for special measures within the educational system. The figures could well be lower – as they frequently have been in the past – or they could be higher if there was serious political and professional will to enhance the standard of achievement of all pupils. Their usefulness is in giving an idea of who is being talked about without resorting to technical language.

Schools, and the education system generally, have responded to the needs of this group in a great many ways, ranging from special schools and other segregated institutions to all sorts of arrangements in ordinary schools. Many ordinary schools have been paying close attention to the needs of their less successful pupils, sometimes hand in hand with having to provide for pupils who might previously have attended a special school. This has led to a great deal of innovation and to a proliferation of educational options. What is necessary now is to take stock and capitalise on this experimentation so that we achieve a coherent educational reform where schools as a matter of course make appropriate provision for all of their pupils.

This book and the series it introduces are concerned with these tasks. The different volumes focus on specific aspects of the necessary school reform and provide detailed discussion of relevant issues and guidelines for practice. This overview volume seeks to lay the groundwork by

- putting the educational options currently available in context
- clarifying the thinking behind emerging developments
- outlining what the proposed school reform entails in practice
- documenting the range of ways in which schools can be supported in the task of educating pupils with difficulties.

Background

Setting the scene

INTEGRATION OR PARTICIPATION?

Many schools have pupils like Peter, Sheila, and the others. Some wish they did not have them and may seek to dispatch them to special schools; some accept them happily enough but do not take them seriously for teaching purposes; some do try to teach them but are hampered by inadequate resources and an unsuitable curriculum; and some – a few – regard them as an integral part of the school's clientele who have the same entitlement to appropriate individual attention as any other pupil in the school and have restructured the entire school accordingly. What most schools share is a growing realisation that they have been failing these pupils and should be doing better by them.

This concern is often couched in terms of integration/segregation. In recent years the issue of integration has come very much to the fore. A major government report referred to it as 'the central contemporary issue in special education'. This focus on integration has arisen out of the special school context: certain children are educated away from their peers, in segregated special schools, and debate has centred on returning them to ordinary schools, i.e. 'integrating' them.

All this attention to provision for those who have difficulty in school is a positive development, and much to be welcomed. It is unfortunate, however, that it is so often expressed in terms of integration, since this is potentially misleading and can divert consideration from the real tasks to be done and the changes to be made. Integration is a shorthand way of referring to a complex and dynamic process and, like many such pieces of shorthand, is open to simplistic and even erroneous uses. What pupils who have difficulties need is *education*, not integration. Placing them in an ordinary school is not an end in itself but a means toward the end of securing them an appropriate education.

A particular problem with integration as a concept is that it is concerned with the pupil rather than the school. It directs attention to the pupil as someone who needs to be integrated rather than to the school which may have to change its practice before an appropriate education can be offered to that pupil. It implies a process where something is done *to* pupils who have difficulties. Integration is *their* problem, and success is measured in terms of how well they have been absorbed into the mainstream rather than how the mainstream has adapted itself in order to accommodate them. A further, related problem with this concept of integration is that it applies to a relatively small proportion of pupils who have difficulties, i.e. those attending special schools. Pupils who have always gone to ordinary schools can hardly be candidates for integration in this sense. They have not been excluded from ordinary schools so that returning them is not at issue.

If there is need of a single concept to sum up the target to which current reforms are directed, it would be better to speak of *participation*. Education is beset with barriers – special school *v.* ordinary school, remedial class *v.* ordinary class, and so on. Some differential treatment is justified, and indeed necessary, since children are clearly different from each other. A good deal of it is not necessary however, and only serves to reinforce the differences. The central concern must be the extent to which pupils who have difficulties participate in, or are excluded from, the educational provision made for their peers. On the assumption that such participation is desirable and to be encouraged, the goal must be to further the participation of pupils with difficulties in the ordinary schooling available to all pupils.

Booth (1982) defines integration in terms of participation – 'a process of increasing participation in the educational and social life of ordinary schools' (page 41). This definition encompasses all pupils whether they be in special schools, in ordinary schools and segregated from other pupils, or in ordinary schools but for whatever reason excluded from some aspect of normal school life. By couching the concept in terms of a process, Booth draws attention to the changes that have to be made if participation is to be a reality. It may be objected that this is an imprecise and relative way of talking about educational provision. We shall see later that, rather than being a weakness, this very relativity is essential in order to avoid spuriously precise language, and to take account of the diversity of schools and pupils' experience of them.

THE DIVERSITY OF PROVISION

One of the first features of the British education system to strike visitors from overseas is the relative absence of central control and the consequent diversity of practice. Local control over education means that almost every aspect of schooling in Britain is subject to immense variation – from age of starting school to arrangements post-16, from length of the school day to class size, from educational expenditure per pupil to the content of the curriculum.

This variation extends to provision for those who have difficulties in school. If anything, it is even more pronounced. The arrangements made for Peter, Sheila, John, Juliet, and Colin give some indication of the different possibilities. We shall see in chapter 7 the full range of educational options in ordinary schools for pupils who have difficulties. There are several options outside the ordinary school as well: special schools, either day or boarding; units organised independently of a school; social services establishments such as community homes with education; and other provision such as home and hospital tuition.

In practice, the range of options is greater than even these listings would imply. First of all, there is overlap between the different categories. For example, individual pupils may divide their time between a special school and an ordinary school. More significantly, the educational provision on offer within a given option can vary widely: one special school can be very different from other special schools, so that the education a pupil will receive is not prescribed by a placement in a special school.

It would be comforting to suppose that this diversity of educational provision matched the range of educational needs – that pupils experiencing a certain kind of placement, e.g., special schools, had certain educational needs in common and that these needs were best met in that kind of placement. The evidence is different. There are many children like John and Colin in special schools, whilst Juliet could well be placed in a unit. The pattern of provision differs greatly from place to place, in response to local policy and practice more than any variation in the pattern of special needs. Some local authorities have a policy of making provision in the ordinary school wherever possible, whilst others maintain an extensive network of special schools. This results in some authorities placing more than double the number of pupils in special schools than others do. Concrete evidence of this comes from an NFER study which found that pupils were being educated satisfactorily in ordinary schools who had commenced their education in special schools and *had they lived elsewhere* would have stayed in special schools (Hegarty and Pocklington, 1981).

To understand this diversity, we have to take account of the historical context of educational provision for those who do not fit into the mainstream pattern. The ordinary school's response to demands for which it was not resourced and that it could not meet was bound up with the emergence of special schools. Whilst this book is concerned with the arrangements made in ordinary schools, the latter are shaped indirectly, and sometimes directly, by special school provision. For this reason the special school context provides an essential backdrop.

Special schools were established early in Britain, with the first schools for the blind being set up before the end of the eighteenth century. Throughout the nineteenth century development was slow: a number of schools for blind and deaf children were opened and, toward the end of the century, some institutions for children with physical handicaps were established. Provision for those regarded as mentally defective was extremely limited and was mostly confined to care and occupational activities. These early initiatives were sporadic, arising as they did from particular local actions and charitable intentions rather than from legislation. The concern was as much to relieve distress and perhaps provide gainful employment as it was to educate.

As universal education spread, the needs of those with more generalised difficulties in learning came into clearer view. The Foster Education Act of 1870, which introduced compulsory schooling, had great expectations of schools. They were to promote learning, develop morals, and prepare the future workers and citizens for a society that was rapidly growing more complex. All this had to be achieved with large classes and few resources, by teachers who were often poorly trained. As the spread of compulsory education introduced more and more children who did not fit the mould, as it were, two main consequences emerged. Firstly, because many of these children failed to learn, school failure on a substantial scale was created. Secondly, these children were often considered to get in the way of class work and so hinder the education of other children. The net outcome was increased pressure for separate provision, whether through special classes in schools or through separate schools.

These developments were bolstered by educational legislation. Initially, legislation merely permitted special provision but gradually came to require it for ever growing numbers of children. Where school boards had merely been allowed to raise funds so as to provide for certain categories of handicapped pupils, the early years of the twentieth century saw such provision charged as a duty on the local education authorities which succeeded the school boards in 1902. The prevailing means for discharging this duty was to establish separate special schools.

The number of special schools increased steadily through the first half of the twentieth century. Major growth came in the wake of the Education Act 1944, along with the post-war expansion in population and school provision. The 1944 Act, and subsequent Regulations, added to local authorities' obligations by extending the range of children's difficulties for which they had to make specific provision. Eleven categories of pupil were defined: blind, partially sighted, deaf, partially deaf, delicate, diabetic, educationally subnormal, epileptic, maladjusted, physically handicapped, and those with speech defects. (These categories, except for diabetic, survived until the Education Act 1981, and indeed are still in common use.) The Regulations prescribed that children who were blind, deaf, epileptic, or physically handicapped should be educated in special schools. Children falling into the other categories might attend ordinary schools if adequate provision was available. In the event, most of the latter also attended special schools.

Ordinary schools were stretched to capacity with the post-war expansion. Both buildings and trained staff were in short supply. Classes were large and schools were not, on the whole, well placed to respond to the individual needs of pupils with difficulties. Special schools with their smaller classes and greater possibilities of individual attention seemed an obvious solution, the more so as a range of apparently suitable buildings was available. The result was a considerable expansion in the number of special schools. This continued up to the early 1970s when the number of special school placements relative to the school-going population stabilised.

AWAY FROM SEGREGATION

One way of viewing the history of special education, then, is to see it in terms of the expansion of special schools. Indeed, one can point to a separate *system* of special schooling that stood alongside ordinary schooling and was quite independent of it. Special schools did not merely deal with different pupils, or at least pupils who were perceived to be different; they also had different curricula, admission procedures, administrative and financial arrangements, and different career patterns for their teachers.

There was a counter trend however. Even as the special school system expand d, the belief was growing that ordinary schools should be doing more to provide for pupils with difficulties. There were two strands to this:

1. Ordinary schools should be providing a more appropriate education for the large number of their own pupils who were failing to achieve very much.
2. Ordinary schools should be capable of educating many pupils who were then attending special schools.

It was the latter strand that got sloganised into the integration debate with its simplistic opposition between ordinary school = good and special school = bad. The reality is more complex. Both strands are facets of the same process of school reform whereby the ordinary school system is restructured so as to provide for a wider range of individual needs. This is discussed in more detail in chapter 5, where the different considerations underpinning each are seen to converge, and in chapter 6, where the characteristics of a school that is responding to a wide range of needs are outlined.

The impetus for reform came from a number of sources. There were two main factors where ordinary schools were concerned. Firstly, school reorganisation and the comprehensive school debate made people look at ordinary schools in a new light. If schools were to cater for all children in the neighbourhood, including the more able 'grammar school' types, should they not be catering for the less able as well? This led to a changed understanding and to new expectations of the ordinary school: the curriculum should be wide-ranging – in particular, it should not be confined to academic learning; teaching arrangements should be flexible to allow for slow progress as well as accelerated learning; and, above all, every pupil should regularly experience success in learning and take from school a sense of personal worth.

In the second place, ordinary schools were clearly failing to meet the needs of many pupils. There was a growing realisation that, apart from those children who were taken out of ordinary schools or never even considered for a place in one because of the absence of suitable provision, ordinary schools were failing many other children as well. Estimates of the number of pupils affected varied widely. Pundits and politicians had a field day. The Warnock Report proposed that about one in six children at any one time would require special educational provision. Others claimed that ordinary schools were failing 50 per cent or even more of their pupils. What was not in dispute was that there was a serious mismatch between the educational needs of large numbers of pupils and what schools were offering them. This was in sharp contrast with the rhetoric of comprehensive schooling, and underlined the need for major reform.

Pressures of a different kind came from the special school sector and the professionals who worked in special education. Three related factors stand out:

1. New ways of looking at children with difficulties.
2. The reaction against categories of handicap.
3. Changes in formal placement procedures.

1. The traditional way of looking at children with difficulties focussed on the children themselves and their inherent limitations. It used a language of defect and handicap and attributed their difficulties to innate characteristics, which were, moreover, relatively stable with time. Grouping pupils with similar characteristics made sense in educational terms, and so special schools were justified. There was a growing realisation, however, that children's educational difficulties do not reside simply in themselves. Home, school, and other environmental factors play a part in creating difficulties. As a result, special schools and other educational arrangements based on traditional groupings had less justification.
2. The reaction against the established categories of handicap was a particular manifestation of this change in perspective. Apart from labelling children in an inappropriate way, these categories implied educational prescriptions. Physically handicapped pupils were considered to have certain educational needs in common, which,

moreover, were different from the educational needs of other children. This is patently not true. There is no direct relationship between physical or sensory impairment and educational difficulties; pupils with similar impairments can have very different educational requirements. Since special schools were based on these categories, and indeed were described as schools for the blind or the educationally subnormal or whatever, the move away from categories of handicap undermined the rationale for these schools and called into question their continued existence – at least in their present form.

3. Developments in placement and assessment procedures provided a further stimulus for change. Traditional arrangements were geared to ascertaining which children were in need of special education and assigning them to handicap categories (and thereby to a particular type of special school). The procedures used had a strong medical bias and were necessarily crude as far as educational programming was concerned.

As psychologists and teachers came to play a greater role, different kinds of information became available and changed the type of placement decision being made. Children's learning difficulties were analysed in greater detail and individual programmes of work were tailor-made for different children. The upshot was that children could not be fitted into predetermined slots to the same extent as before. New patterns of provision had to be devised and made available in a flexible way. This could be done – and sometimes was – within special schools but there was no necessary reason for this apart from the greater concentration of some of the requisite expertise in special schools. The better articulation of children's educational needs constituted a new dynamic that changed both special schools and ordinary schools.

Yet further pressure for change came from the perceived deficiencies of special schools. The justification of special schooling was not merely that it made up for the failures of the ordinary school sector but that it offered a superior education to some children and ensured that they were given the best possible start in life. The trouble was that a growing number of people just did not believe this. And if the claimed advantages were not present, what was left was a collection of drawbacks and restrictions.

Numerous charges were levelled at the special school. It offered a narrow curriculum – too much stress on basic literacy and numeracy and too little specialist input from subject areas such as history or science. The presumed expertise in dealing with and teaching pupils with difficulties was frequently not present: the proportion of special school teachers with specific training for teaching their target clientele was small. As for the pupils, special schools imposed a damaging isolation. They were separated from their neighbourhood peer group and out-of-school friends and, in the case of residential schools, from family as well. Deprived of opportunities to associate with normal age peers, they tended to acquire untoward patterns of behaviour and become launched on 'handicap careers'. In summary, special schools neither gave a good academic grounding nor prepared young people adequately for life after school.

Each one of these charges could be refuted by individual schools – and would be done so with vehemence by some! Certainly, there are very good special schools that give young people with difficulties an excellent start in life and any ordinary school would be stretched to the limit in order to do as well in an integrated setting. Equally, there are some very bad special schools that, if anything, add to the learning difficulties of their pupils. What mattered, however, was not the existence of particularly good or particularly bad special schools – it would be surprising if there was not a wide variation in practice, just as there is with ordinary schools. What did matter was that many special schools were *perceived* to be offering an inferior education. Special schooling was having to justify itself and in the eyes of many was failing to do so. This then led to further pressure for change.

Some broader influences may be noted as well. First, the experience of successful innovation can be a powerful force for change. A number of reports on mainstreaming practices abroad reached this country. Visitors to Denmark, Sweden, and the United States came back with glowing accounts of the ways in which pupils with difficulties were being educated in ordinary schools. Though some of these accounts were exaggerated or based on misperceptions, their net effect was to add to the case for change. More immediate pressure came from the experience of successful innovation in this country. Whilst reports from Wisconsin or Uppsala could be dismissed as irrelevant to or not feasible in the British context, it was less easy to discount practice in Bradford or Derbyshire. In fact, there was a good deal of local innovation in this country, much of it unknown outside the immediate locality, but, as reports spread, they had a significant effect. Their demonstration that different forms of provision were possible and that pupils with very considerable difficulties could be educated in ordinary schools proved very important for many people who were unswayed by theoretical or ideological arguments.

A final context for change was provided by the civil rights movement. This flourished in the United States in the 1960s as blacks and others suffering discrimination agitated publicly, and campaigned to remove the restrictions that beset them and limited their participation in the mainstream of society. Other groups, including the handicapped, followed suit. A major focus of campaigning was to remove the barriers in employment, housing, and general participation in the community that hived people off into ghettos of disadvantage. Education came under scrutiny as well, both on its own account and on account of its contribution to disadvantage in other areas. The practice of segregated special schooling was regarded as highly problematic, and therefore a prime target for reform. It violated the child's right to live free of unnecessary restrictions, to attend school with neighbourhood peers and to receive an appropriate education within as normal an environment as possible.

WHERE ARE WE NOW?

The so-called integration movement has been gathering momentum in this country for ten years or more now. Section 10 of the Education Act 1976 provided an initial legislative boost which was confirmed by the Education Act 1981. (Chapter 3 looks at the legislation and its requirements in detail.) Numerous activities highlighted the importance of integration in the public as well as the professional mind – articles extolling the virtues of integration appeared everywhere from popular magazines to daily newspapers, pressure groups campaigned, conferences and lectures proliferated, and inservice education for teachers increasingly focussed on integration. At times it seemed as if the only topic of consequence in special education was integration, and it was only a matter of time before special schooling withered away and all children were educated in ordinary schools.

This clearly has not happened and shows no signs of happening. What then has been achieved? Have the rhetoric and the campaigning and the legislation made a difference to how special education is delivered? Or are we just using different labels and deluding ourselves into thinking that there has been real change?

If we take special schooling first, a mixed picture emerges. On the one side, some local authorities have significantly curtailed their use of special schools and have switched resources accordingly to the ordinary school sector. There has been a growing realisation that some groups of children previously deemed to need special schooling, e.g., those with physical handicaps and those with visual impairments, have little need of it when their individual situation is looked at; many, indeed, fare perfectly well in an ordinary school with little special support. A considerable number of special schools have created links with nearby ordinary schools whereby individual pupils can divide their time between the two schools; flexible arrangements are made to enable each pupil to have the programme judged most appropriate for him or her at any given time. (Chapter 9 examines the extent of these links and the various forms they take.)

As against all this, the use made of special schooling has grown in some localities and sectors. There has been an expansion in schools catering for pupils with emotional and behavioural difficulties. On a

national scale, the proportion of pupils attending special schools
has not declined. The actual numbers have come down in line with
the drop in the schoolgoing population, but the proportion has been
virtually static – at about 13 per 1000 since the early 1970s. (This is
the number of pupils aged 5–15 in special schools expressed as a
proportion of the total school population in the same age range.)
Most recently, concern has been voiced about an apparent slight
upsurge in placements. It must be remembered, however, that the
available figures are inexact: the basis on which figures are collected
at local level is not uniform, and significant developments, such as
the schools linking arrangements referred to above, are not
adequately reflected. Moreover, comparisons over time are
rendered extremely difficult by changes in the way that official
statistics have been collected, and by changes in the underlying
population and the need for special arrangements for sections of it.

As far as ordinary schools are concerned, two contrasting trends can
be identified, though the balance of advantage seems far clearer. The
pressure to make better provision for pupils with difficulties led –
paradoxically – to greater segregation in some cases as special classes
and units were set up on a self-contained basis. Pupils in such units can
end up being as isolated from mainstream peers as if they attended a
separate special school. Larger units in particular run the danger of
becoming mini special schools, suffering all the disadvantages of being
located in an ordinary school yet having none of the advantages –
autonomy, concentration of expertise, links with external services, and
so on – of being a free-standing special school.

More positively, significant improvements are being brought
about in ordinary schools. There is a greater awareness of a wide
range of pupil needs and a growing commitment to meeting them.
This is reflected in the changes being effected in school organisation, staffing, curriculum and teaching approach. Another paradox
is evident here where changes introduced in order to accommodate
a small number of newcomers to a school who have considerable
learning difficulties turn out to have as much relevance to pupils
with difficulties who are already at the school. In many ways the
major beneficiaries of the integration movement are these latter
pupils who have always attended ordinary schools but have not
received an education appropriate to their needs.

Since this is widely acknowledged to be a sizeable group, nothing
less than a thoroughgoing reform of schools will suffice. If the
reform is to be achieved, major professional development of
teachers and other workers concerned with schools is necessary.
Attitudes must change, new knowledge and skills have to be
acquired, so that the requisite curriculum frameworks can be
translated into relevant learning by pupils. The purpose of this book
is to chart the dimensions of this reform so that, in conjunction with
the other books in the series, it can help to bring it about.

—3—
What the law says

Teachers are not normally concerned with the detail of educational legislation. It is a long way removed from the classroom and may appear to have little bearing on their work. Had this book been written five years ago, it probably would not have included the present chapter. Recent years have, however, seen major legislative changes affecting both the way in which pupils with difficulties are perceived in schools and the nature of the provision made for them. Whilst this legislation deals largely with the small group of pupils who have marked difficulties in school, it does provide a framework for the education of all pupils with difficulties. For this reason it must be regarded as an essential part of the context within which the reform of the ordinary school will be achieved. The chapter first summarises the main provisions of the new legislation and then looks at the effects it is having.

THE 1981 LEGISLATION

Major changes to the law on special education were introduced in 1981, though not implemented until 1st April 1983. Prior to that time, pupils whose education presented difficulty – often referred to as handicapped pupils – were covered by the Education Act 1944 along with all other pupils. It had been evident for some time that the existing law was unsatisfactory: it was based on an outmoded concept of handicap; it lacked adequate procedures for assessing and recording children's specific educational requirements; and it did not have a sufficient orientation toward making suitable provision in ordinary schools. There had been an earlier attempt at legislative reform in the Education Act 1976 but this was limited and in the event never implemented. In the meantime, the Warnock Commission, established in 1974, was sitting. The Commission was a major focus of interest during the long gestation period of its report. This appeared in 1978 and served both to crystallise and further the debate on special educational provision and to provide the basis for legislative action.

The Education Act 1981 amended key sections of the Education

Act 1944 and became the central law governing special education in England and Wales. It was supplemented in 1983 by a set of Regulations that amplified the law on assessments and how they were to be conducted and recorded. In addition, a circular of guidance – Circular 1/83: Assessments and Statements of Special Educational Needs – was issued in 1983; this is not part of the law but its recommendations have considerable force. (Corresponding legislation has been enacted in Scotland to take account of the differences in the Scottish educational system and to ensure that equivalent changes take place there.)

The basic thrust of the new legislation can be described under four headings:

1. The concept of special educational need.
2. Provision in ordinary schools for pupils with special educational needs.
3. Identification and assessment of pupils with special needs.
4. The use of Statements to make a formal record of pupils' special needs.

1. Special educational needs

The conceptual basis of the Act is provided by the notion of 'special educational need'. This is discussed in detail in chapter 4 of this book and only the formal legislative usage need be considered here. The term was not new, though its use and the novel way of regarding children with difficulties that it entailed had been slow in gaining ground. What was notable about the Act was that it adopted, for legislative purposes, a relative, provision-oriented concept in place of the fixed, child-based concept of handicap that preceded it.

Under the Act, a child is deemed to have special educational needs if he or she has 'a learning difficulty which calls for special educational provision to be made'. This necessitates two further definitions, viz. 'learning difficulties' and 'special educational provision'. Children have a learning difficulty if they have a significantly great difficulty in learning than the majority of children of their age, or if they have a disability that either prevents or hinders them from making use of the educational facilities generally available to age peers. Special educational provision is defined as 'educational provision which is additional to, or otherwise different from, the educational provision made generally for children in schools maintained by the local education authority concerned'.

The Act makes a critical distinction within the group defined in this way. Some children will be the direct responsibility of the local authority in the sense that they have 'special educational needs which call for the local education authority to determine the special educational provision that should be made for them'. This implicitly defines two groups of children with special educational needs, those whose education remains the responsibility of the school, and those for whom the local authority must determine provision. The Act has nothing to say on the severity or the nature of the needs that would place a child in one or other group, though it is clearly implied that the two groups comprise those with lesser and greater needs respectively. In practice, they are being interpreted loosely as the 18 per cent and the 2 per cent referred to in chapter 4.

With the exception of children in maintained nursery schools, the two groups are dealt with very differently under the Act. There is relatively little on those pupils whose education remains the responsibility of the school: schools are charged to 'use their best endeavours' to ensure that they receive an appropriate education in an integrated setting, as spelt out below; teachers must be told about the special educational needs of pupils in their school and made aware of the importance of providing appropriately for them. Most of the legislation is given over to the group of pupils whose educational provision must be determined by the local authority. Their special needs must be formally assessed, and very detailed procedures are laid down for conducting assessments and communicating the results to those concerned.

Children at nursery schools are treated somewhat differently. The local authority is responsible for ensuring that appropriate provision is made for *all* children with special educational needs in nursery schools, regardless of whether formal procedures have been invoked or not. In most cases a formal assessment would not be conducted, though the opportunity to do so is there if the authority considers it necessary or a parent requests it.

2. Provision in ordinary schools

It is a major principle of the Act that children with special educational needs should be educated in ordinary schools to the greatest extent possible. This principle is not enjoined in an absolute way nor is it designed to lead to the rapid elimination of the special school system. In this respect it stands in sharp contrast to the corresponding legislation in countries such as Italy where there has been a radical switching of resources from special schools to ordinary schools. It has also failed to go as far as many people in this country would have liked since it appears to place very little pressure on local authorities who are content to maintain the status quo.

The Act does mark a radical departure however. Under the 1944

Act, local authorities were expected to provide for handicapped pupils in special schools and were merely *allowed* to do so in ordinary schools if circumstances permitted. The 1981 Act exactly reverses this situation: the ordinary school is declared to be the normal place of education for all pupils, and special schools are only to be used when necessity so dictates. In the context of British educational legislation this is a significant shift. Absolute prescriptions are not necessary in order to effect far-reaching change or to redirect resources in major ways. The fact that the Act contains many apparent loopholes in respect of integration does not mean that it is thereby impotent in respect of bringing about change. Change is already taking place, albeit slowly, and time will tell to what extent it is significant.

What exactly does the Act have to say regarding provision in ordinary schools? What are the exclusion clauses that might enable a school or authority to drag its feet? Section 2 is the relevant part of the Act. This is where the duties of both authorities and schools are laid down. If a child is deemed to require special educational provision the local authority is required, subject to certain conditions, 'to secure that he is educated in an ordinary school'. Likewise, if a child with special educational needs is being educated in an ordinary school, there is a duty to ensure, again so far as is compatible with certain conditions, that 'the child engages in the activities of the school, together with children who do not have special educational needs'. Broadly, the same conditions, or exclusion clauses, apply in both cases. They are four in number and are worded as follows:

> The conditions are that account has been taken ... of the views of the child's parents and that educating the child in an ordinary school is compatible with
> a) his receiving the special educational provision that he requires;
> b) the provision of efficient education for the children with whom he will be educated; and
> c) the efficient use of resources.

These conditions have attracted a good deal of attention. They can be interpreted in very different ways. Some welcome them as sensible caveats to guide implementation, others deride them as emasculating escape clauses that justify inaction. A more neutral view is that they are simply a gloss on the underlying requirement to make provision in ordinary schools in that they merely elaborate how it has to happen: no one would seriously advocate that children should not receive the special educational provision they require or that resources should not be used efficiently. As noted above, these conditions must be viewed in the context of educational legislation in general and its relationship to how change actually occurs in British schools. On balance, this context would suggest that the Act does make a difference; whilst the exclusion clauses may lessen its bite, they do not leave it toothless.[1]

3. Identification and assessment

The Act and the ensuing documents paid a great deal of attention to identifying children with special educational needs and assessing them in order to establish what their educational needs actually are. Different procedures are laid down for the two groups described above. Assessment should take place within the school for those pupils whose educational provision remains the responsibility of the school. This should be a continuous process, designed to feed into class teaching and the monitoring of progress. It should be conducted initially by the class teacher and extended progressively, as necessary, to the head teacher and specialists from outside the school. When external specialists become involved, they should work closely with the teacher. Parents should be involved also and kept fully informed at every stage.

When there is a likelihood that the local authority will determine the special educational provision to be made for a pupil, a formal assessment must be conducted. Very detailed procedures are laid down for the conduct of such assessments. Parents must be involved in specified ways and have guaranteed rights of appeal. If the outcome of an assessment is that a child is deemed to require special educational provision and that a formal Statement of Special Educational Needs must be made, this will specify the child's special educational needs and the provision that will be made to meet these needs.

These procedures are discussed in detail in a handbook produced by the Advisory Centre for Education (Newell, 1983) and will only be outlined briefly here. Local education authorities are required to identify all children who may need special educational provision. Parents also can initiate the process by requesting an assessment for

---

[1]These are the conditions that apply in respect of *attendance* at an ordinary school. With regard to *participation* in the normal activities of the school, the same conditions (a), (b), and (c) apply; additionally, such participation must be 'reasonably practicable'. The Act does not explicitly require parents' views to be taken into account here, though failure to do so would go counter to the spirit of the Circular on assessment. Also, the general principle laid down in the Education Act 1944 still holds, viz. that 'pupils are to be educated in accordance with the wishes of their parents'.

their child; authorities must comply with this and arrange an assessment unless they consider it unreasonable. (In the event of a refusal parents can appeal to the Secretary of State.) When a local authority decides to assess a child, it must inform the parents both of its intention to do so and how exactly it proposes to act.

In order to make an assessment, the authority must obtain educational, medical, and psychological evidence and 'any other advice which the authority considers desirable in the case in question'. This advice must be in written form and must relate to the child's present and likely future educational needs and how they are to be met. The requisite educational advice will be obtained, through the head teacher, from the child's class teachers in the case of a child at school. Medical advice will naturally be obtained from a medical practitioner and psychological advice from an educational psychologist. The latter will normally be designated by the respective authorities for doing this work and should be familiar both with assessment practice and with local provision. Account must also be taken of any representations made by parents. The outcome of the procedure is either that special educational provision is not deemed necessary or that it is, in which case a formal Statement must be made. Again, parents have the right to appeal to the Secretary of State if a Statement has not been made.

4. Statements

The requirement to have a formal Statement of Special Educational Needs is a significant new departure. It guarantees a public, explicit record of the child's special educational needs and details of how they are going to be met. Specifically, a Statement must include:

- the authority's assessment of the child's special educational needs
- the requisite educational provision 'in terms of facilities and equipment, staffing arrangements, curriculum or otherwise'
- the type of school the authority considers would be appropriate and – if a particular school is in mind – its name
- any necessary non-educational provision such as might be provided by health or social services authorities and
- all the written advice obtained by the local authority in making the assessment as well as any representations or evidence submitted by parents.

Local authorities are required to review Statements every 12 months and inform parents of any changes made. Parents must be consulted over any proposals to amend a Statement. Detailed procedures are laid down for parents to appeal against the special educational provision set out in the Statement.

If a young person is still the subject of a Statement of Special Educational Needs at 14, the Disabled Persons Act 1986 requires that a further assessment be conducted when he or she leaves full-time education. This is to determine the needs of the person in respect of the statutory services provided by the local authority. It is intended to secure access to appropriate services on the basis of identified need.

IMPLEMENTING THE ACT

Now that the legislation is in place, we have to ask what difference it makes. Has it delivered what was expected of it? Are pupils with difficulties receiving a better educational deal than before? Have the sceptics who saw no real change in prospect been confounded, or proved right by subsequent events? Where there have been changes, would they have come about if the Act had not been passed?

It is too early to give definitive answers to these questions. The Act only came into force in April 1983 and needs time for full implementation. Whilst a number of authorities were geared up to implementing it, even anticipating some of its major requirements, others were slower off the mark and have experienced difficulty with the necessary resourcing arrangements. There have, too, been other pressures for change in recent years, and it would be simplistic to expect a single explanation for the changes that have taken place. There are some pointers to early implementation, however, at two different levels. First, there are the specific procedural changes, notably concerning assessment, required by the Act. Secondly, there are the more general changes in special needs provision where legislation may have played a part.

The specific changes are most evident in relation to assessment and statementing procedures. Circular 1/83 (DES/DHSS, 1983) sets out a very detailed framework within which the assessments laid down in Section 5 of the Act are to be carried out. An entire issue of *Special Education: Forward Trends* (December 1983) was given over to the implications of this assessment framework for the local authority, for the school as a whole, for parents, and for the various professionals involved – psychologists, speech therapists, paediatricians, psychiatrists, and teachers.

The legislation has undoubtedly had an effect here as authorities seek to conform to the requirements of the Circular. The procedures are explicit and detailed, to the extent of specifying who should be involved, in what way, at which stage, how many days should elapse between certain stages, and what should happen at each point where disagreement might arise. Not every authority is implementing the procedures in full, but many have made significant progress. Large numbers of pupils are receiving Statements, and their parents are accordingly being informed about the special educational provision being made for them.

The result of all this is a considerable expansion of both administrative and professional services in local authorities. Some authorities have appointed Statementing Officers, and most are dealing with a far greater volume of paperwork in connection with these pupils. The expansion in school psychological services documented in chapter 8 can be attributed in large measure to the proliferation of Section 5 assessments.

Information on the operation of the equivalent procedures in Scotland has been collected by Thomson et al. (1986). The Education (Scotland) Act requires authorities to maintain a Record of children's needs as opposed to the Statement in England and Wales; there is a corresponding set of procedures for conducting assessments and maintaining the Record. In the study, data were collected on the procedures as seen by a sample of professionals dealing with pupils with visual impairment.

The procedures were perceived to have a number of disadvantages, stemming principally from too much formality and bureaucracy. Psychologists felt that the formal procedures obstructed good clinical practice. Education officers and head teachers regarded the amount of administrative time and paperwork involved as excessive. This echoes the comment in Adams (1986) referring to the Act in England and Wales as leading to 'warm photocopiers and paper everywhere'. The extended timescale imposed by the various stages built into the procedures could delay access to provision.

Particular criticism was made of the initial letter to parents informing them that a formal Record of needs was under consideration for their child. These letters often confused and disturbed parents. Their official, legalistic tone could be intimidating and served little other purpose than to add to parents' burdens. This concurs with Rutherford's (1986) view of the Recording procedure in Scotland after two-and-a-half years' experience. The letter to parents was seen as cumbersome and alienated many of them – 'there is no doubt that the whole tone of the letters is an abomination and interferes with the development of a constructive relationship between parents and professionals' (page 36).

The principal advantages in the new procedures were seen to relate to parents. Parents now had formal rights, specifically in respect of consultation. They obtained a copy of the document containing the professional assessment of their child. This strengthened their hand in dealing with the professionals who simultaneously became more accountable and more precise in what they said about children. Some believed that there was greater professional accountability as well: the fact that professional assessments and prescriptions were open to scrutiny put pressure on staff to collaborate and attend more closely to the range of services that were actually available.

On the broader front, there has been a great deal of change and development in special needs provision in recent years. This pertains very much to the general arena of implementation of the Act. There are numerous factors at play here, as outlined in chapter 2. The Act is only one of a variety of causes, but it is clear that it is having an impact at this general level.

First, there is the language used to describe pupils who have difficulties. (The next chapter discusses in detail why the traditional language of handicap was unsuitable and has to be set aside.) There had been a growing realisation that change was necessary but it was not until the arrival of the Act that the old language became displaced to any significant extent. Its formal adoption of the term 'special educational need' and the associated concepts has not merely affected how we talk about pupils who have difficulties in school; it has also contributed to a significant change in how these pupils are perceived and what sort of educational provision is judged appropriate for them.

At the level of services, the Act has helped in the expansion of special needs provision. Later chapters outline developments in local authority support services, the growing links between special schools and ordinary schools, and the proliferation of inservice education. These developments stem from various sources and would be taking place to some extent whether the Act was passed or not. The Act has given them an undoubted fillip, however, both by focussing attention on special needs provision and by facilitating the acquisition of resources.

A recurring complaint concerns the lack of information about the Act and its implementation. In a study of parental perceptions of professionals, Sandow and Stafford (1986) found that parents of children assessed for special educational needs knew very little about the Act. Parents were interviewed in 1984/85 about their contacts with professionals at a time when the production of formal Statements of special needs was beginning in the two authorities concerned. A majority of the parents had not heard of the Act, even though all had recently had their child assessed under it. Of those who had heard of it, many did not know what a Statement was or were unaware of the appeals procedure and the requirement to hold an annual review. Over two-thirds of the parents said that no one had explained the procedures involved in deciding on their child's future needs.

A survey by the Spastics Society in 1984/5 found many gaps in the information about the Act provided to parents by local authorities (Rogers, 1986a). Authorities were asked for copies of the material they published for parents giving details of their policies and arrangements for identifying, assessing and providing for special educational needs. Approximately two-thirds of authorities responded. Whilst some of the materials were excellent, many were judged deficient on numerous counts – no mention of parents' right to request a formal assessment of their child, nothing on the requirement to hold an annual review, no information on the appeals procedures. It should be pointed out that this information was collected at a relatively early stage in the implementation of the Act and that a number of authorities were planning to develop the information they provided.

A further survey found that the information procedure for professional staff was more homogeneous in quality (Rogers, 1986b). All 66 authorities responding had guidelines which were aimed at head teachers, teaching staff and educational psychologists. Some also issued guidance to school governors and to health and social services professionals. The emphasis was very much on assessments and Statementing procedures, and the guidelines issued tended to rely heavily on Circular 1/83 and other official documents.

There are authorities that take their information duties very seriously. A good many have developed clear and comprehensive guidelines and ensure that officers are available to meet parents who have queries. Rogers (1986a) cites some of these. Several authorities have published detailed statements of their policy and provision for special needs. Thus, the ILEA report *Educational Opportunities for All?* sets out the authority's review of provision for special educational needs and gives a great deal of information on options available and procedures to follow (ILEA, 1985).

Kramer (1985 and 1987) describes how his authority – Derbyshire – ascertained views on its special needs provision in the wake of the Act with a view to improving both the provision and information about it. Parents and voluntary bodies as well as professionals were consulted as part of a wide-ranging review of services. Particular attention was paid to the new arrangements for multiprofessional assessment. The majority of parents expressed satisfaction with the new procedures but the exercise did serve to pin-point areas where improvements could be made.

Another common .complaint is that it is a 'no-resources' Act, introduced at a time when educational expenditure was being cut. Schools and authorities are expected to expand provision in major ways but have not been given the means to do so. This is a particular bone of contention in the secondary sector where schools are having to contend with a number of major initiatives such as the Technical and Vocational Education Initiative (TVEI) and profiling, the reform of the examination system and the pressures created by high levels of youth unemployment. Provision for special needs must take its place alongside these developments, and it has been a source of great regret to many people in the service that the Act did not provide resources to back the reforms it called for.

The fact that resources are not guaranteed by the Act has almost certainly hindered its implementation, both because of the absolute scarcity of resources and because of the negative attitudes created by the legislators' apparent failure to acknowledge the resource implications of their mandates. Notwithstanding this, significant progress has been made. Later chapters document what has been achieved in spite of the pressure on resources. Gipps, Gross and Goldstein (1987), in a study of changing models of support for pupils with special needs in primary schools, found that the impact of the cuts in educational expenditure on the support services was much less than anticipated. Remedial teaching and provision had been under severe pressure at the beginning of the 1980s. By the time of the study in 1983/84 this pressure was found to have eased, and special needs provision in authorities was expanding. The 1981 Act was seen as an essential lever for action in this regard, and without it the momentum for developing provision would not have been maintained.

A DES-funded study has been examining the implementation of the Act in local authorities in England. Interim findings (from the University of London Institute of Education) paint an uneven picture, complicated by the difficulty of deciding whether a particular development came about as a result of the Act or for other reasons. A few specific points may be noted:

- there was found to be general support for replacing the handicap categories with the concept of special educational needs. The importance of environmental factors in determining a pupil's needs was recognised, though the application of the Statementing procedures placed a predominant emphasis on defects within the child
- the proportion of children with Statements varied widely between and within local authorities

- there was an increased concern for accountability, but the Statementing procedures appeared to have increased the involvement rather than the participation of parents in decisions about provision for their children's needs
- parents' participation was limited to some extent by the lack of relevant information about the statutory procedures and available provision
- there was strong evidence of higher expectations among parents about effective support for their children with special needs
- in general, local education authorities reported they had increased the proportion of their budget allocated to special needs provision: it was uncertain, however, whether they could sustain this in the face of increased demands and decreased funding
- the Statementing procedures were absorbing a large amount of staff time
- the function of Statements was still uncertain with regard to the communication of information among those responsible for meeting the pupil's needs.

In summary, the Act has yet to be fully implemented. There have been numerous problems – too much bureaucracy, excessive paperwork, too little information to consumers, great variations in practice. Some authorities have taken the Act to heart and have been very successful in finding the necessary resources to implement it, whereas others have been moving far more slowly. There has been progress however. The diversity of provision, which is endemic within the British educational system, should not deflect attention from the achievements that have been made. The successful practice of some authorities demonstrates that the Act does provide a framework for developing services for pupils with special needs in an effective and comprehensive way.

—4—

Special educational needs

There has been very little about handicap so far in this book. Pupils who would commonly be called handicapped are being referred to as 'pupils with difficulties'. This chapter is given over to a further apparent circumlocution, viz. 'special educational needs'.

This may look like studied vagueness or an excess of delicacy. 'Pupils with difficulty' is so all-encompassing as to be virtually meaningless. When we talk about handicapped pupils everybody knows what we mean, whereas virtually every pupil has a difficulty of one kind or another. This circumlocutory language smacks of academic pedantry and a reluctance to face facts. If Colin, in the earlier examples, is physically disabled, then he *is* physically disabled and there is nothing to be gained from ignoring the fact. Roundabout phrases do not alter the underlying realities of incapacity and failure.

The time has clearly come to look at the reasons for this linguistic footwork. The burden of this chapter is that the old language of handicap is seriously defective. Its conciseness comes from crude simplification, and the apparent precision is spurious. Its reflection of the underlying realities is actually a gross distortion of them. So, whilst the language of special educational needs may be infelicitous and imprecise, it corresponds more closely to the learning situation of individual pupils. It is based on a truer understanding of why they have difficulty in learning, and educational programmes grounded on it are more likely to be successful. Moreover, it provides a framework for considering in a coherent way the educational needs of a very much larger group of pupils. Handicap considerations tend to apply to the small proportion of those with marked difficulties and to imply – mistakenly – discrete provision for them.

THE LANGUAGE OF HANDICAP

What exactly is wrong with the language of handicap? It has served for many years. The system of categories of handicap established in 1945 helped in securing systematic provision for a considerable number of children whose needs had hitherto received only sporadic attention. It provided a framework for assessment and provision that lasted for close on 40 years – a period which saw great expansion, in terms of both resources and sophistication, in services for the group. Moreover, the language of handicap is widely used in other countries. It establishes a common frame of reference, and is not generally regarded as being particularly problematic.

The difficulties with the language of handicap are of three kinds, concerned respectively with: the individual child; the school; and the education system as a whole.

The individual child

As far as the individual child is concerned, four considerations may be noted. Firstly, the language of handicap is unduly, and unhelpfully, negative. Secondly, it is muddled and often wrong in what it has to say about individuals. Thirdly, it has limited relevance to the consideration of teaching and learning needs and can indeed be a misleading guide in respect of them. Finally, it imposes labels on children that stigmatise them and can harm their self-concept.

Take first the negativity. The focus is on what the child cannot do, on disabilities rather than abilities. It speaks of 'the handicapped' as a group characterised by their inability to do certain things. This is unsatisfactory on two counts. The fact that people cannot see or are confined to wheelchairs may not be the most important thing about them; indeed, it may be relatively insignificant in their lives. Regardless of this, the blindness or the physical handicap is continually thrust to the forefront by the language of handicap so that the handicapping condition dominates how everything else about them is perceived.

The case of Franklin D. Roosevelt, President of the United States of America from 1933 to 1945, throws an interesting sidelight here. Crippled by polio in midlife, he was virtually confined to a wheelchair thereafter. His public appearances were carefully stage-managed, however, so that he was never seen being carried. His disability could not be concealed but its effects were deliberately minimised so as to appear less than they actually were. This was presumably to ensure that the image of disability did not loom too large in people's minds and conflict with the desired image of the presidency. In other words, Roosevelt was a president who happened to be physically handicapped – if anybody presumed to mention it; he was not a physically handicapped president.

A second consideration here has to do with negative definitions in general. Negative definitions are frequently uninformative and can be misleading in their apparent specificity. By their nature they depend on a context of meaning established elsewhere. This is straightforward if the latter is clear and specific – as, for example, with foreigner and virgin. Where the underlying context is not well defined – as perhaps with atheist or uncultured – the negative definition is at least as imprecise, and it may be quite difficult to attach any clear meaning to it.

Handicap tends to fall between these, or to oscillate from one to the other. Visual impairment is clear enough if we spell it out in terms of the inability to read print of a given size under specified lighting conditions, but what about mental handicap? This could be elaborated in terms of difficulties in learning and social competence. So many qualifying conditions have to be laid down, however, regarding the content of learning and areas of competence, the manner and context of teaching, motivation, and prior learning experiences, that a shorthand phrase such as 'mentally handicapped' becomes of little use. (The oddness of the usage 'non-handicapped' can be noted here. It is a double negative, used to specify those who do not possess certain negative characteristics! They are not unable to hear normally, they do not fail at learning, and so on.)

A second difficulty with the language of handicap is that it is muddled and prone to error. It conflates things which are in reality very different. Blindness, educational subnormality, and maladjustment are all regarded as handicaps despite being very different from each other especially as regards their relationship to the learning process, and children who are blind, educationally subnormal, or maladjusted are all seen as belonging to a common handicapped group. This lumping together of children whose situations and needs are so different leads to much confusion and misunderstanding.

Blindness is a physical condition with certain educational implications, which can generally be spelled out fairly precisely. Educational subnormality is the state of being educationally subnormal, i.e. of failing to learn within the normal educational provision offered to age peers and needing some different educational input. In the case of those labelled severely subnormal, this failure to learn is sometimes attributed to 'mental handicap' by apparent analogy with physical handicap: learning is a matter for the mind, and if the learning is not taking place there must be something wrong with the mind. It is rarely clear precisely what is wrong, however, since it is seldom possible to point to specific brain damage or neurological deficiency that directly explains the failure to learn. Maladjustment is an even more elusive concept since it is essentially relative. It is a failure to adjust to particular situations or to behave according to expected norms. Situations and expectations vary however, and what is acceptable in one case may not be acceptable – thereby constituting maladjustment – in another.

As well as being muddled, this way of looking at children's difficulties in learning is based on a fundamental misconception. It sees the difficulties as being rooted in the child and disregards environmental factors that may be significant in creating difficulties. Educational failure is regarded as the result of internal defects, whether these be plainly evident as in the case of physical and sensory handicaps, or invisible as in most other cases. This leads to a static view of potential where a child's likely achievement is limited by innate and relatively enduring characteristics.

The third difficulty is probably the most damning. Even though special education and special schools in particular have been based on the categories of handicap for many years, these categories have strictly limited relevance to the planning and delivery of educational provision. Pupils with similar handicaps may have very different educational needs, so that knowing which category a pupil slots into may not help much in actual teaching. Thus, pupils who fall into the partially hearing category vary greatly in the amount of useful hearing they possess and in the extent to which they learn to make use of it. In any case, even if two pupils have the same level of reduced hearing, their education will be affected by a whole range of factors, just as happens with normally hearing pupils. This is not to say that the fact of sensory impairment or other factual information implicit in the allocation to a category of handicap should be ignored when drawing up educational programmes. It is rather to stress that this is only one strand of information amongst many, and not necessarily the most important one. Teachers have long recognised this, of course, even in handicap-defined special schools, as is evident in the widespread commitment to devising individual programmes of work that match a pupil's particular strengths and needs.

A final difficulty is that labels become attached to pupils. Inevitably, these are pejorative, and they stick. What they do is to isolate a particular aspect of the person and magnify it in the common perception and in the individual's self-perception so that he or she is viewed exclusively in terms of that aspect. Thus, the child becomes educationally subnormal or physically handicapped first and an individual second. This would be bad enough if the labels were essential and served a useful purpose. In fact, as we have seen, they are neither. They contribute little to educational programming and can seriously affect children's self-concepts.

The school

As far as the school is concerned, there are two problems with the language of handicap. First, it leads to a definition of special schools in terms of single handicaps – schools for the blind, schools for the educationally subnormal, and so on. Whilst this may be administratively convenient, and has certainly been effective in securing resources, it cannot be an acceptable long-term strategy. We have seen already that children's educational needs are no more than partially established by reference to handicaps. This means that supposedly single-handicap schools in reality have pupils with a wide range of needs. In principle, this should not be a problem so long as the school recognises the situation and is equipped to deal with the diversity of needs. In practice, there are problems. Schools are resourced in terms of their assigned handicap and tend to see themselves as concerned in a major way with it. As well as tending to create an ethos of handicap, this can be a barrier to focussing on children's educational needs rather than on their handicaps.

The second problem is that, even with well-defined categories of handicap, children do not slot neatly into just one category. Consider a boy who is categorised blind and educationally subnormal, and assume that he is to be educated in a special school. Should this be a school for the blind or a school for the educationally subnormal? Or should schools be set up for those who are both blind and educationally subnormal? And for those who are deaf and educationally subnormal? And physically handicapped and educationally subnormal? What if the boy in question was maladjusted as well? It is easy to see that this would lead to an unwarranted proliferation of types of special school. Were special schools not to disregard their assigned categories in such cases and respond to the needs of pupils as they present themselves, this is where the logic of allocation by handicap would take us.

The system

There are some more general problems with the language of handicap that have to do both with the way in which children and young people with difficulties are perceived and with the provision of support services. First, this language accentuates their difficulties to the extent that individuals are defined in terms of them. This, in turn, establishes a sharp distinction between two groups – the handicapped and the non-handicapped. Everything about the former is viewed from a handicap perspective and, in particular, education is organised for them on separate, handicap-related lines.

This divide between 'handicapped' and 'non-handicapped' leads to a second problem, namely that pupils with lesser or less obvious difficulties do not receive the extra attention that they may need. The range of difficulties that pupils experience in learning is very great: they may be short term or related to particular aspects of the curriculum; they may be present at specific stages of development only; or they may be generic and long-lasting. The variation is such as not to be encompassed readily in categories. The result of using categories of handicap, then, is that attention and provision are concentrated on the small number that fit into the available categories, and the very much larger number of other pupils with difficulties receive far less attention.

WHY CHILDREN HAVE DIFFICULTY IN LEARNING

Why do children fail at school? Why do some children adjust

happily to life at school, concentrate on what they are about, develop interests and skills, and become mature young adults, whilst others fail to engage in the life of the school, learn very little and leave school ill-equipped to lead an independent adult life? The reasons are as many as there are children of course – it is all too easy to forget that children are individuals and the story of each one's learning growth is unique.

The multitude of reasons can be grouped into three broad but interlocking sets: individual factors of the type associated above with the language of handicap; environmental factors; and school system factors. The first two sets of reasons are relatively familiar and need not be discussed at length here. The school's role in creating learning difficulties is less well recognised, and it is important to understand it clearly if relevant reform is to be carried out.

Individual factors must not be ignored. The numerous difficulties with the language of handicap shown above should not be taken to imply that there are no factors within the child that inhibit learning: this would be to replace one extreme view with another. Impairments of sight and hearing, of speech and physical function, cannot be disregarded as far as learning is concerned. The fact that there is not a direct or invariant link between a given impairment and a particular kind of learning difficulty does not mean that there are no links. Likewise, children manifest differences in learning rate and emotional resilience which affect how well they learn. These individual differences may well reflect innate factors even if the precise causal link is seldom established.

The child is a social being as well as an individual and is a member of various social groupings – family, neighbourhood, social class, ethnic group, language community. This is the arena in which environmental factors come into play. These factors are not in themselves the direct cause of learning difficulties but rather provide a context in which certain development should take place within the child. If this development does take place the child is set to grow in learning in a way that will be regarded normal; if it does not the child is likely to experience learning difficulty.

The key components of this development as far as schooling is concerned are skills, knowledge, and attitudes. The child needs appropriate stimulation and learning experiences in order to develop intellectual capacity and learning skills. Certain items of knowledge must be acquired since some learning is cumulative, with later learning dependent on earlier facts and insights being mastered. Finally, attitudes to learning are of key importance and if they are not promoted in the child's non-school environment school learning is likely to be attended with difficulty.

THE SCHOOL AS A SOURCE OF LEARNING DIFFICULTIES

The most pervasive source of children's school difficulties is the schooling system itself. School failure can, after all, only occur in schools and could not exist without them! This is not as glib as it sounds. Schools define the activities and the standards by which pupils' achievement is marked. They also set the benchmarks for failure. This is dramatically illustrated by the experience of some young people when they leave school: the difficulties of adjustment and learning that characterised their school careers become insignificant and, bereft of the opportunity for regular failure, they turn into young adults indistinguishable from their peers.

It should not come as a surprise that schools create learning difficulties. The long-running debate on school effectiveness, for instance, shows that schools do make a difference. It may be difficult to pin-point the critical factors, but it is clear that pupils receive a better education in some schools than they would in other schools. If this is so, it must also be accepted that some schools make poorer educational provision than others. Most studies of school effectiveness have paid little attention to low-attaining pupils. One that did was by Rutter et al. (1979). It found that examination results for the least able pupils varied significantly between schools. Amongst the reasons put forward by Rutter to explain the differences in school outcomes were the degree of academic emphasis, the availability of incentives, and the extent to which pupils were able to take responsibility.

Another perspective on the school's role in creating learning difficulties comes from considering the school as an agent of social change. Some historians and social theorists see it as inevitable that schools should create such difficulties. Education is a form of social control, designed to fit children into a limited number of life slots, and as universal education spread it did not respond to children's individual situations. (It is unlikely that it could have done even if the intention was there.) All children of the same age were assumed to be the same for purposes of instruction, despite the obvious fact that they were not, and given the same educational treatment. Those children who did not fit should have highlighted the inadequacy of the system. That was neatly avoided, however, by defining the 'misfits' as the problem: they became school failures who were tolerated as non-productive members of the ordinary school or cast out into a special school.

How, in practice, do schools create learning difficulties? The curriculum is at the heart of the matter. This is where pupils achieve, and have their achievement acknowledged; it is also where they fail and learn that they have failed. For present purposes the curriculum can be taken as a combination of what is taught (and why), the means by which it is taught, and assessment procedures.

A major problem is the widespread reliance on traditional school subjects in order to specify curriculum content. This is particularly so in secondary schools where the public examination system has direct influence on the curriculum. The effect of this subject focus is that too much emphasis is placed on acquiring knowledge, especially factual knowledge that can be reproduced on paper. There is nothing wrong with knowledge acquisition, but excessive attention to it creates problems for pupils with special needs and makes it less likely that they will derive any benefit from teaching.

Firstly, it sets up hierarchies where such pupils will generally come bottom. When science, for instance, is seen as a body of knowledge to be mastered, it is difficult to conceive of teaching it other than in terms of success and failure. Some pupils can cope with chemical valency and specific gravity, and others cannot. The more of a defined body of knowledge a pupil masters, the more successful he or she is. This is fine for some pupils, but for many their main acquisition is a public and regularly reinforced sense of failure.

Secondly, this focus on knowledge acquisition makes the task of curriculum modification more difficult, and indeed sets limited to what can be done. If the objective is that pupils amass facts, modifying curriculum content essentially means reducing the number and complexity of the facts to be mastered. There is little room for developing alternative approaches whereby pupils of whatever level of academic ability are given a sense of what 'doing science' means. This entails learning facts, of course, but much more besides. Pupils must have structured experiences which generate the sort of question that leads to scientific insight, which highlight the limitations of common sense, and which show the need for measurement and other systematic procedures.

A potent illustration of the effects of an inappropriate curriculum is given by Hargreaves (1982). He is concerned with the dominance in comprehensive secondary schools of the academic curriculum – what he terms the cognitive–intellectual domain. Far less attention is given to other domains that are also important in education – the aesthetic–artistic, the affective–emotional, the physical–manual, and the personal–social. Hargreaves cites himself as an example of somebody who was competent in the cognitive–intellectual domain but a distinct failure at woodwork; in no sense was he a school failure, however, since 'my conspicuous failure had been drowned in a sea of moderate success'.

A very different situation faces pupils who are weak in the cognitive–intellectual domain and strong, for instance, in the physical–manual one. To dramatise their overweening sense of failure he sketches a nightmarish scenario where pupils such as him are confined to a school where the traditional emphases are overturned and academic subjects give way to the physical–manual domain.

In this nightmare my secondary school's timetable is dominated by periods of compulsory woodwork and metal work, gymnastics, football and cricket, drawing and painting, technical drawing, swimming and cross-country running. Sandwiched between these lessons, but only in thin slices, appear welcome lessons in arithmetic and English, in French and history. Some of these, however, cease to be available to me after the third year; they clash with the more important subjects of technical drawing and gymnastics which I need for higher education and a good job. I enjoy most lessons very little; I am bored and make little effort in areas where I seem destined to fail. The temptation to 'muck about' in lessons, and even to truant, is almost irresistible. My friends soon matter to me much more than anything else in school and our greatest pleasure is in trying to subvert and mock the institution which we are forced to attend for five long years. I don't think my teachers, who seem so strong and clever with their hands and feet, really understand me at all. Quite often they are kind, but I know they look down on me and think it's all rather hopeless in my case. I'll be glad to leave school.

Hargreaves (page 64)

The school curriculum is not geared to the full range of potential achievement. Some areas of achievement are played down or even ignored, and children whose only excellence is in these areas become unwitting failures. The predominant focus remains an academic one, frequently quite narrowly so, with the result that success and failure at school are defined in terms of this single aspect of achievement.

As well as creating failure, a narrow school curriculum can breed disaffection. Older pupils especially have some idea of the options open to them when they leave school. They also have views – which can be more or less well-informed – on the relevance of the curriculum to these options. If their conclusion is that it has little relevance, it is not surprising that they reject school whether by overtly disruptive behaviour or absence or refusal to engage in learning activities.

SPECIAL EDUCATIONAL NEEDS

What has emerged so far is that the language of handicap is problematic and in many ways grossly unsuited to talking about the education of pupils with difficulties. It is pejorative and isolating; it gives a misleading basis for planning appropriate educational provision, frequently, indeed, distorting the pattern of provision; and above all it implies and reinforces a mistaken understanding of the nature and causes of learning difficulties. The difficulties children experience in school derive from different sources. Sometimes there is a direct link with innate handicap-related factors, though it is often not possible to establish such links in an educationally useful way. More often, the difficulties arise from environmental or school-related factors, or from the interaction within a pupil of different kinds of factors.

The response to this situation in recent years has been to set aside the language of handicap and speak rather of 'special educational need'. This has been enshrined in legislation and in official language generally, though it is still a long way from gaining everyday currency – partly, no doubt, because it is novel and cumbersome, but also because it entails new ways of thinking that are neither familiar to nor accepted by all workers in the field. It is precisely because of these new ways of thinking and the far-reaching changes in practice they imply that the new language canot be dismissed as a passing fad or as academic pedantry.

The term 'special educational need' was adopted by the Warnock Report as central to its thinking and many of its recommendations for action were couched in terms of it. The concept was not new of course. It had been used by various authors previously but had not dislodged the language of handicap to any great extent. The post-Warnock debate was to change that. The Report coincided with an upsurge of interest in the education of children with difficulties, an upsurge it helped to swell and structure. Legislation was imminent, educational provision was being reorganised, a spate of writing from research reports to pop journalism appeared and debate proliferated.

All of this conspired to place the notion of special educational need on centre stage. A more significant development still was the passing of the Education Act 1981, which, as we have seen in chapter 3, gave it a specific legislative significance. Previous legislation spoke of handicapped children, who had defects that required special measures to be taken. The defects were characteristic of the children, and the challenge was to make the most appropriate provision possible. The 1981 Act recognises, through its focus on special educational needs, that the provision itself may be contributing to pupils' difficulties, and that reform of provision rather than simply improvements to it is what is required. Many of the practical proposals of the Act follow from this recognition.

A RELATIVE CONCEPT

The concept of special educational need is essentially relative – to the level of difficulty experienced by other children and to the kind of educational provision available in a given locality. The Warnock report specified that it should be seen not in terms of any particular disability that a child may have but 'in relation to everything about him, his abilities as well as his disabilities – indeed all the factors which have a bearing on his educational progress' (3.6). We have already seen that the legislative definition of special educational need involves two further concepts, namely learning difficulty and special educational provision, each of which is characterised in a relative way. Children have a learning difficulty if they have a significantly greater difficulty in learning or in using common educational facilities than others of their age. Special educational provision is educational provision which is *extra* to what is available for the generality of pupils.

A practical consequence of this is that whether a child is deemed to have special needs or not depends in part on where he or she lives. If two local authorities maintain different levels of educational provision, they will, in effect, be operating different criteria in deciding who has special needs. More concretely, a child may have special educational needs in one school but not in another. This can be because of different standards of performance and behaviour or because of different levels of educational provision.

This is most vividly demonstrated in the case of pupils who have emotional and behavioural difficulties. Various studies have shown significant differences between schools in their capacity to provide adequately for these pupils. The incidence of 'maladjusment' varies widely even between schools that have similar catchment areas. Likewise, there is considerable variation between schools in the number of pupils they exclude, or seek to exclude, because of 'disruptive' behaviour.

This relativity may be startling at first sight but it should not be. It is neither new nor out of tune with current thinking on the measurement of individual differences. Take the measurement of intelligence as a case in point. In the past IQ has been regarded as a fixed and dependable measure, and has indeed had widespread use in defining individuals as educationally subnormal or mentally retarded. There is a growing realisation however that intelligence tests are far from absolute and that the assignment to categories based on them is often fallible.

A brief technical digression is necessary to show why this is so. An individual's score on an intelligence test, or any similar test, is derived by comparing the number of correct responses made by that person with other people's responses. (Technically, it is a norm-referenced test, where scores do not relate to independent criteria, as for instance in graded music exams, but only to norms or standards established by representative performance.) To facilitate the use and interpretation of tests, the pattern of responses obtained from a large, representative sample is used to establish score guidelines – average score, and better and worse scores at various levels. A subsequent individual score is interpreted in terms of these guidelines.

The difficulties arise when measures such as this are taken out of context and used on their own. They are then likely to acquire an absolute significance that can be very misleading. Tom has an IQ of 100 and is therefore normal, Dick has an IQ of 70 and is therefore educationally subnormal, Harry has an IQ of 130 and is therefore gifted. The simplistic use of IQ scores out of context is particularly unfortunate in the case of children from ethnic minority or other socioculturally different groups, since in their case the interpetation of IQ scores is even more indirect. If a child from such a group scores 100 in an IQ test, all this means is that he or she is performing at the level of the average child from the indigenous group. If we can identify sociocultural differences that make the test harder for children from that background, this score might emerge as *equivalent* to the performance of an indigenous child scoring 110 or 115.

In fact, recent efforts to improve assessment practice for such children have highlighted the relativity of IQ scores. One of the best known procedures here is associated with the work of Jane Mercer in California. Along with colleagues she has devised a battery of tests known as SOMPA – System of Multi-Pluralistic Assessment (Mercer and Lewis, 1979). This is based on estimating learning potential. It assumes that IQ is a valid measure of learning potential for 'normal' children, but for many it is an indirect measure at best and must be adjusted in the light of the environment in which they live. So, the battery contains in addition to an intelligence test a range of instruments designed to build up a comprehensive set of information on a child – family and sociocultural background, health, and school experiences. This information is used to adjust the child's IQ score so that it better reflects that child's learning potential.

TEASING OUT THE CONCEPT

The language of special needs is gradually, albeit slowly, becoming established. Whilst many still find it easier to talk of handicapped children, ESN pupils, and so on, this is only to be expected. Old habits and ways of speech die hard and it would be naive to expect the language of handicap to disappear instantly. The language of special needs is here to stay however, particularly as it has been incorporated into educational legislation. It may be helpful, therefore, to tease out some of the implications of the concept of special educational need.

Firstly, the thrust of the concept is toward provision. Special educational needs only make sense in a context of provision – and the inadequacy of what is regarded to be normal levels of provision. Under the 1981 Act what establishes a child as having special educational needs is that he or she requires special educational provision. It does not talk about innate characteristics of the child but about the schooling that he or she receives and how he or she responds to it. Even 'learning difficulty', which is part of the formal definition, is defined in terms of the child's ability to respond to the teaching provision available. The net result is that special educational needs are provision-led rather than child-led.

Secondly, special educational needs cannot be categorised easily. There is no ready equivalent of the old categories of handicap. Limitations of sight, hearing, and so on still have relevance, but their impact is not uniform as far as education is concerned and they do not provide a basis for classifying children's need of special provision. What special educational needs have in common is the inadequacy of ordinary schools in respect of a wide range of pupil difficulties. An alternative category system, then, would have to describe systematically the different ways in which schools are actually inadequate. An outline description of schools' inadequacies does seem possible but it is difficult to see how this could be broken down in the systematic detail that a category system would require.

Thirdly, and following from the preceding points, this way of looking at special educational needs puts the major responsibility on the school. It is only within schools that the individual's special needs emerge in specific form and can be defined in operational terms. Equally, the educational provision appropriate to meeting these needs can only be specified by reference to the educational provision of a particular school. Schools must therefore be alert to their responsibilities and be in a position to discharge them if they are to meet children's needs and indeed refrain from adding to them.

It should be acknowledged that there are difficulties with the notion of special educational need. Firstly, there is a logical oddness about the term, specifically in the relationship between learning difficulty and special educational provision. A child is said to have special educational needs if he or she has a learning difficulty *that calls for* special educational provision. In normal usage this would imply that there are different kinds of learning difficulties and that only some, viz. those requiring special educational provision, lead to a child having special educational needs. This might appear reasonable were it not for the way in which learning difficulties are defined: a child has a learning difficulty if he or she has a significantly greater difficulty in learning than the majority of children of his or her age and so on. Presumably, all such children require some special educational provision and all, therefore, must be regarded as having special educational needs. This would suggest that the learning difficulty is at the core of the concept and that special educational provision is simply an explanatory gloss, i.e. a child has special educational needs if he or she has a learning difficulty, in which case there is need of special educational provision.

A second difficulty is possibly more serious. For all that the concept is couched in terms of provision and the educational environment, it ends up with an undue focus on the child. Take as an example two schools that are identical in all respects except that one permits wheelchair access and one does not. A child that is confined to a wheelchair cannot make use of the 'educational facilities … generally provided' in one case but can in the other. So the child would have a learning difficulty and therefore a special educational need if living in the catchment area of one of the schools but not if living in the catchment area of the other. Apart from the anomaly, what this language is doing is transferring a feature of school architecture into something the child *has*. The net effect of this could be to frustrate one of the major intentions of the new approaches. Rather than shifting attention from the child who has difficulties to the educational environment in which these difficulties are created or exacerbated, it runs the risk of replacing one child-based form of description – categories of handicap – with another.

In summary, special educational needs are here to stay. We have seen that the language of handicap is beset with major difficulties, whether the concern is with the individual child, the school or the education system as a whole. The critical factor is that it is based on a limited and frequently mistaken view of why children have difficulty in learning. The language of special educational needs attempts to address these problems. Whilst it is not totally satisfactory it has acquired legislative status and is gradually coming into general use. Its focus on provision and its acknowledgement of the relative nature of children's difficulties mean that it corresponds more closely to the learning situation of individual children, and educational programmes based on it are more likely to be relevant and effective.

Toward A New Kind Of School

—5————————————————

Integration and school reform – the case for change

Why should pupils with special needs be educated in ordinary schools? If it comes to that, *should* they in fact be educated in ordinary schools? What reasons are there to justify tinkering with, even dismantling, a well-established system of special schools in favour of *ad hoc* arrangements in often unreceptive ordinary schools?

These questions are not fashionable. Integration is the order of the day, and questions like these jar with the rhetoric that surrounds it. Yet they must be faced. Integration is not a self-evident state of affairs, nor does it have universal support. Many people with long experience of special education – parents and pupils as well as professionals – remain strongly opposed to it, and there are some indeed who regard it as educationally disastrous.

This points to the need for a hard look at the case for integration. Is it just one more bandwagon for jumping onto, or are there sound educational and other reasons for making the far-reaching changes it entails? And are there different considerations where different groups of pupils are concerned? Is it easier, for instance, to integrate pupils with learning difficulties than those who have emotional and behavioural problems?

There has been no shortage of debate, not to say controversy, about integration in recent years. Many would say that there has been too much talk and too little action as it is. This does not obviate the need for a dispassionate look at the arguments however. There is little enough consensus on the form integrated provision should take or on how extensively the principles of integration should apply. Witness the enormous diversity of practice from one local authority to another and the uneven pattern of progress toward more integrated forms of provision. Witness also the different views as to which pupils, at what age and with which special needs should be integrated. The benefit of a deliberate scrutiny of the reasons for and against is that integration can then be adopted – or not – on the basis of reasoned argument, that the complexities and compromises necessitated by integration are clearly in view, and that the requisite changes in schools are seen within the context of the whole school.

In this chapter a distinction is made between pupils with problems in learning who are already in ordinary schools – the so-called 18 per cent – and pupils in special schools, since different considerations hold for the two groups. The 18 per cent are only discussed briefly here since the arguments are relatively straightforward and the issues arising are taken up throughout the book. Where the two per cent are concerned, the key questions have to do with desegregation, and so it is necessary to look at the reasons for and against special schooling. These turn out to be inconclusive, and in the end desegregation emerges as a moral issue revolving round the right to participate in normal society. This leads the way to a convergence of the two sets of issues in a common school reform.

THE 18 PER CENT

The integration debate has been beset with misunderstanding and lack of clarity. As the initial concern with desegregation gave way to improving ordinary schools, there developed an unfortunate tendency to regard the two processes as identical. Certainly, they are closely connected and feed into each other, but they are not the same and much confusion has resulted from using the term 'integration' in an unqualified way to refer to both.

Desegregation in the narrow sense of removing pupils from special schools obviously applies only to those who are in a special school or might be considered for a special school placement. It is a non-issue as far as the larger group of those with special needs is concerned since they are already in ordinary schools.[1] For these the questions inspired by integration are rhetorical or strictly practical ones.

The rhetorical questions are questions such as: Should ordinary schools be providing an appropriate education for all the pupils that attend them? Should pupils who have difficulty in learning in an ordinary school receive appropriate extra attention according to

---

[1]This group is often referred to loosely as 'the 18 per cent'. The origins of this designation lie in the Warnock Report's estimation that up to one in five children would require some form of special educational provision during their school career. Popular debate made much of the 20 per cent of children categorised in this way. Of this group some two per cent were generally supposed to have difficulties so serious as to warrant special schooling. (In point of fact the proportion of children in special schools is rather less than two per cent.) By subtraction we arrive at 18 per cent of children requiring some special educational provision but attending ordinary schools. The estimate is imprecise but it does provide a convenient shorthand designation.

need? Even though the reality of educational practice is often disappointing and many schools devote disproportionately fewer of their resources to those whose problems in learning are greatest, the principle of appropriate education for all in unexceptionable and does not need justification.

These issues have long been aired in the comprehensive school debate, and it is worth noting why that debate has, for all its egalitarian rhetoric, ignored pupils with learning difficulties until very recently. Comprehensive schools were conceived as providing for all the children in a neighbourhood. The emphasis, however, was on social egalitarianism and on achieving in schools a broad social mix that reflected the social composition of the local community. This led to a near-fixation with social class. The principal effort was to ensure that schools were comprehensive in social class terms, and that children were not excluded from nor consigned to particular forms of schooling on the basis of their parents' socioeconomic status.

This egalitarian motivation may have been a necessary condition for effective school reform but it has certainly not been a sufficient one. Over and above their role in creating a social melting pot, comprehensive schools also sought justification in terms of educational and psychological criteria. Schools should be providing a wider curricular range and should be delivering it more flexibly; teaching methods should be taking better account of pupils' learning needs; and the whole effort of schooling should be geared more closely to developing individual potential. In other words, there was need of major curriculum reform where the egalitarianism of the social reformers was matched by curricular initiatives that were no less radical.

In the event, the requisite curriculum reform did not take place on anything like the scale required. If it had done, the likelihood is that serious curricular attention would have been given to pupils with learning difficulties far sooner, and initiatives like the Lower Attaining Pupils Programme would have emerged in the 1970s rather than the 1980s. What happened in practice often was that the old goods were decked out in new trimmings. As Hargreaves (1982) and others have pointed out, comprehensive schools tended to model themselves on grammar schools rather than on secondary modern schools, and few attempted to fuse the two traditions or set off along new curricular directions. Comprehensive schools were to be 'grammar schools for all'. As new schools they had to prove themselves, and there was a natural concern over standards. In key respects these remained the standards of grammar school education. The traditional cognitive–intellectual curriculum continued as the dominant element, reinforced by the status assigned to it within comprehensive schools and by the public examination system.

The upshot of all this was that the rhetoric of equal opportunity stayed as rhetoric where many pupils were concerned. Pupils whose development was slow or who had difficulties in learning had neither adequate nor equal access to the curriculum. A system of remedial education was developed for them but this was often, as Smith (1985) has said, 'an ambulance service for the casualties of our educational system rendered accident-prone by a curriculum based on rigid streaming' (page 4). So the rhetorical questions are seen to have more force. In particular, they lead to two sets of practical questions: 'What does an appropriately reformed curriculum look like?' and 'How do we set about achieving it?' These questions are taken up in later chapters and indeed form the core of this entire series of books.

SPECIAL SCHOOLS OR NOT?

At one level the issue is very simple: special schools were necessitated by either the inability or failure of ordinary schools to educate certain groups of pupils, and they should continue in existence just as long as it takes ordinary schools to secure adequate educational provision for these pupils. In practice, it is not quite so simple. Special schools are not a short-term expedient that can be lightly set aside once their job is done and they are declared to be no longer necessary. They are an established part of the pattern of educational provision and have acquired a life and a momentum of their own. So, even if their job *is* done – and it is far from easy to make an irrefutable case – consideration must be given to the problems of dismantling a well-tried system.

It is not just a matter of shutting down individual special schools and transferring their pupils and staff to ordinary schools. That may turn out to be necessary, but any closures must take place within a context of system change. Special schooling is a sub-system of the broader education system, and also intersects with other systems such as the health service and the voluntary societies. In addition to school buildings and teaching arrangements, it encompasses ascertainment and assessment procedures, teacher career patterns, curriculum development, involvement of the school psychological service and other agencies, fundraising activities, and a distinctive school ethos and pattern of pupil–adult relationships. Changes to any one component of the system are likely to have repercussions for all the others, so that shutting a special school has wide-ranging implications for the pupils concerned and the educational provision they receive.

The case for special schools is complex and multifaceted. There are numerous aspects to it, and each has to be analysed in its own terms. Of the various components of schooling, the following relate to the concerns most frequently voiced: How does the academic progress of pupils in special schools compare with the progress of equivalent pupils in ordinary schools? Is there a differential impact on pupils' social and emotional development? Are there differences in the curriculum range typically available in the two settings? Do parents have a preference for one or other setting? What about costs – is either setting cheaper or more cost-effective than the other?

Some of these issues are taken up below. Parents and costs are discussed in chapters 11 and 12 respectively. In each case attention is drawn to the comparative questions: 'What do we know about parental preference, and the cost of provision, as between special schools and integrated arrangements?' and 'How dependable is the information available to us?' Here we look at the comparative questions arising in relation to academic attainment, social and emotional development, and the curriculum range.

Academic achievement

The traditional way of evaluating integration programmes, particularly in the United States, has been to look at pupils' academic attainments. The basic questions are: 'How do pupils' school achievements compare across different settings?' and 'If pupils move from a segregated setting to an integrated one, are they likely to get better or worse academic results?'

Academic learning is a major part of what schooling is about, and it is certainly appropriate that pupils' academic achievements should be a criterion in deciding between different educational settings. It is well to be aware, however, that the available research evidence – and there is a great deal of it – does not give straightforward messages or point in a single direction. Many comparative studies have been done in the United States, as well as a few in this country. Close examination of these studies shows that their findings do not consistently favour a particular kind of educational placement: some have found that pupils had higher levels of achievement in integrated settings whilst others, using similar measures of achievement, have found precisely the opposite. (See Hegarty and Pocklington, 1981 for a detailed overview.) In other words, if the goal is to maximise pupil learning, the research evidence does not arbitrate for or against integration.

It is not difficult to see why the research findings are inconclusive. Consider the question being asked: Given a group of pupils in a particular educational setting, would their achievements be different if they were moved to another setting? This is a simple question to ask but answering it is far from simple. (Incidentally, how often are such questions asked in mainstream education, whether about schools themselves or about particular aspects of schooling?) The question is a hypothetical one and, in a sense, is unanswerable. Pupils can only experience one setting at a time and, whilst we can measure what they learn in it, we can only speculate as to what they would have learned in a different setting; if they move to that setting, we can measure what they learn there but then do not know what they would have achieved in the first setting had they continued in it.

There are two possible approaches to this difficulty. The first is to make use of control groups. If we cannot tell how a particular group would have fared in a setting different from the one it actually experienced, it is nevertheless possible to expose a similar group to the alternative setting and examine how it fares. This procedure is widely used. It is clear that it depends critically on the extent to which the two groups are similar. In practice, the procedure is to take certain measurable characteristics of the first group and ensure that the second, or control, group matches it in terms of these characteristics. If the two groups are adequately matched in terms of the educational settings being investigated, they can be regarded as equivalent for purposes of comparison. This means that it is possible to compare the two settings as distinct from the two groups.

The matching process is the key to this whole enterprise. It is also its potential weakness. Unless the two groups really are equivalent, any comparison is going to reflect a mixture of groups and settings, and it may well be impossible to disentangle their relative effects. There is inevitable compromise here. Two groups of schoolchildren can never be equivalent in other than a limited sense. What matters is that they be equivalent in terms of their receptivity to a set of educational experiences. The studies of interest conventionally match groups in terms of age, sex and IQ – and little or nothing else. This is where the matching, and with it the rationale of control group studies, break down. There are many other factors besides these that bear on pupils' responses to an educational programme. Prior learning experiences, motivation, relationship to the teacher, and home background all affect how well pupils learn. If these factors are not taken into account, any matching carried out it likely to be incomplete and consequently the validity of any comparisons will be limited.

A second approach to the comparative problem is based on extrapolation from past performance. This relies on building up a detailed knowledge of individual pupils, knowing how pupils with particular patterns of impairment and learning difficulty develop over time, and being able to estimate how individuals would progress if they continued in an established setting. This could then provide a baseline for comparing performance in a different setting. Thus, if we can predict what a pupil with a given hearing loss would attain in a year's time assuming he or she stayed in a special school, we can compare this with the actual attainment in an integrated setting.

In practice, this approach has hardly been used, nor is it difficult to see why. The predictions rest on two legs: models of pupil learning to guide prediction on their future development; and detailed knowledge of pupils' learning situations. There are many factors known, or suspected, to influence how pupils learn. We do not understand these factors well enough to be able to construct very exact models of pupil learning. This is all the more so for pupils with special needs because of the ways their impairments may interact with the other factors.

Even if a workable model has been constructed, it is essential to have detailed knowledge of individual pupils and their learning situations in order to use it to make predictions. Conventional academic tests provide some of the necessary information but not all of it. There are important facets of pupil behaviour and response to learning situations that are amenable only to teacher observation and judgement. These are encapsulated in teachers' *tacit* knowledge of their pupils. Whilst teachers are sometimes very skilled at predicting how well their pupils will progress, it can be difficult to translate their expectations into precise statements about specific levels of achievement.

Social and emotional development

Children's social and emotional development is not the primary business of schools but it is easy to see why they have to concern themselves with it. Children enter school as immature infants and leave as young adults. School is a major arena of social experience during these formative years and exerts a good deal of influence on the course of children's social development. It is therefore legitimate to scrutinise different schooling arrangements in terms of how well they promote social and emotional development.

This issue tends to become highly charged where pupils who have difficulties are concerned. The extent to which they develop in social and emotional terms has become a touchstone of integration for many people. Those opposed to integration say that pupils with difficulties run the risk of being socially isolated in ordinary schools and having their emotional difficulties compounded, have no opportunity to excel in peer terms and do not receive the specific grounding in independence that good special schools provide. As against that, others point to the 'natural' social situation of the ordinary school where pupils with difficulties can learn to become part of the larger community they will eventually join, where untoward social behaviour tends to become eliminated through the pressure of pupil interaction and where there are many opportunities for essential social learning.

There have been numerous studies attempting to establish the relative superiority of ordinary schools and special schools in terms of social and emotional development. These have generally taken the form of controlled comparisons along the lines of the studies of academic achievement referred to above. They have focussed on different aspects of development – independence, maturity and display of socially acceptable behaviour.

What emerges from these studies? Is there a particular setting that is most conducive to social development? Unfortunately, the research evidence is no more definitive nor specific than it is in the case of academic achievement. The findings do not consistently favour either special schools or ordinary schools, and those who would advocate one or other gain little support from these studies where social and emotional development is concerned. It should be noted that the same limitations pointed out in respect of academic achievement studies generally apply to these studies as well. All the methodological problems of control groups and extrapolation from past behaviour arise and make the interpretation of findings just as tentative.

There is another type of research study, however, that does point in a particular direction. This involves a group of children who might have gone to special schools but are actually in ordinary schools and whose special and emotional development has been monitored over a period of time. If their development follows a normal pattern this is of significance in its own right without having recourse to comparison. Special schools and ordinary schools are not equivalent forms of placement, with free choice between them: pupils go to a special school only if there is some significant difficulty attaching to an ordinary school placement. So, if pupils' levels of development and behaviour in integrated settings are shown to come within normal expectations, that alone constitutes a strong justification for integrated placements. We do not, after all, subject the social and emotional development of the majority of pupils to scrutiny in this way or require their school experience to be compared with hypothetical other placements.

There are methodological problems here too. What constitutes 'normal', and how do we measure it? Normality is a relative concept. It is also used imprecisely, encompassing a wide range of behaviour. As a result, it is neither easy to define nor to measure. This is particularly problematic in the case of pupils with difficulties. A physical or sensory impairment can introduce a further level of relativity: what is normal for a wheelchair user or somebody who is partially sighted is not necessarily normal for another person. It can, moreover, be difficult to establish what the equivalent behaviour would be in cases where impairments impose certain restrictions on behaviour.

One study that sought to address these issues was conducted at NFER (Hegarty and Pocklington, 1981). It took samples of pupils in ordinary schools and examined their social and emotional development. All had special needs of one kind or another, ranging from physical and sensory impairments to moderate or severe learning difficulties. Information was gathered in three main areas:

1. maturity, including self-confidence, independence, and adjustment to handicaps;
2. relationships – with peers and with adults;
3. behaviour and personal presentation.

Summarising the findings, the authors say:

> There was a broad consensus among teachers, parents and pupils themselves that they had benefited in terms of social and emotional development from taking part in the integration programmes. There were gains in self-confidence and independence, while being in an ordinary school promoted a realistic acceptance of the individual's handicapping condition .... Negative relationships such as teasing were comparatively rare. The incidence of untoward behaviour and bizarre mannerisms was considered to have greatly lessened.
>
> (Hegarty and Pocklington, page 454)

To the extent that these findings are valid, they constitute an endorsement of the integration arrangements made for the pupils in question. It is not necessary to know how they would have fared in other settings. In an ideal world, more information is always desirable, but in the real world of educational provision and choices about it, this degree of information is already more than is often available to guide decision-making.

Curriculum

Another focus of comparison is the curriculum. This subsumes both academic learning and social and emotional development but is much broader. The curriculum is being understood here as the school's total effort to achieve certain objectives and so takes in content, teaching/learning methods and assessment procedures. The empirical questions are broader as well. The interest is in schools and what they offer rather than the achievement or status of individual pupils. Any comparisons made relate to school and system variables rather than to pupil variables.

Two aspects of the curriculum are frequently picked out as relevant to the integration debate: breadth of content and teaching expertise. Small schools are necessarily restricted in the range of subject they can offer. Since special schools are almost invariably small, this is a major limitation, particularly at secondary level. Not only is the number of subjects small but particular areas of the curriculum tend to be sparsely represented. There are, for instance, relatively few science or music specialists in special schools. (Ordinary schools too experience shortages. There is currently a scarcity of teachers of mathematics, science, design, and foreign languages.)

Whilst these considerations might seem to be an unambiguous argument in favour of ordinary schools, the reality is less straight-forward. Pupils with special needs in an ordinary school do not always have access to the full mainstream curriculum and some-times, indeed, are more restricted in their curricular experience than they would be in a special school. Consider a large comprehensive school offering, say, 20 subjects. No pupil in the school is going to study the full range, and there are at least three reasons why pupils with special needs may be confined to a very limited selection.

Firstly, the sheer complexity of the timetable in a large school imposes its own limitations; it can be difficult to accommodate groups or individuals whose programmes of work differ signifi-cantly from the norm. This is very often the situation with pupils who have special needs, with the result that their programmes are more restricted than they might be in a special school. A related consideration is that option choices in the later years of secondary schooling are necessarily limited. Only a set number of pupils in a year can take a given option. This means that schools have to make choices or set admission criteria. Frequently this is done in ways that effectively exclude pupils with special needs from certain sought-af-ter options and channel them toward less popular ones.

Secondly, pupils with special needs, particularly if they have moderate learning difficulties, are often fed a heavy diet of basic work in language and number so that there is less time for other areas of the curriculum. An NFER survey of provision for slow learners in secondary schools found that the curriculum provided for slow learners was often different from that provided for others in the same year group. Less than half of the schools surveyed offered the full range of subjects to slow learners in the first three years of school. The subjects most frequently omitted were modern languages and science (Clunies-Ross and Wimhurst, 1983). This narrowing of the curriculum on offer tends to be more pronounced the greater the pupils' learning difficulties are perceived to be. The reasoning behind it presumably is that literacy is so important in adult life that everything else must take second place to acquiring it.

Finally, there is the question of mediating subject matter so that pupils with special needs are *actually* exposed to it as distinct from being present in a lesson where it is taught. Sitting in a science lesson is not necessarily to do science. Experience, vocabulary, and concepts must all be geared to the recipients' present stage of development. This can be difficult enough to achieve anyway but becomes doubly so when teachers are not aware of the gap between their usual teaching practice and what some pupils with special needs require. If subject specialists fail to take these pupils seriously for teaching purposes, their participation in specialist lessons is nominal – and a waste of everybody's time.

So much for breadth of content. Ordinary schools may have the potential to offer a far wider range of curriculum than special schools, but in practice they often fail to do so. A great deal of careful effort is necessary in order to translate this potential into real curriculum offerings.

This turns the focus onto the second aspect of the curriculum referred to above, viz. teaching expertise and the extent to which pupils are engaged in appropriate learning activities. Special schools would seem to hold the balance of advantage here. Special school staff are expert in special needs and have experience in teaching pupils with learning difficulties. They are familiar with the patterns of learning difficulty, know what curricular materials and other resources are available, and are versed in drawing up and implementing individual programmes of work. Above all, they have small classes and can give pupils individual attention. All of this means that the special school can become as it were a learning collective where the entire staff cumulate an understanding of special needs and a competence in teaching pupils with difficulties. The knowledge and expertise acquired by one teacher in one class are readily shared with colleagues. Between them they encounter a wide variety of pupils and possess a large pool of expertise.

The ordinary school can respond to this in two ways, first by claiming that the above is an idealised picture of the special school, and then by pointing to some particular teaching advantages possessed by the ordinary school. Certainly, there are special schools that could hardly be described as centres of excellence and where the idea of staff forming an interactive learning community is difficult to imagine. Not all teachers in special schools are expert in special needs or possess the requisite teaching and programme planning skills. The most recently available figures indicate that only a quarter of special school teachers have received specialist training in special needs. It must be acknowledged that this greatly underestimates their professional competence. Special school staff can legitimately point to the experience and the sharing with expert colleagues that special schools make possible. In addition, there is the growing volume of inservice training that is enhancing professional development in special schools and ordinary schools alike.

What of the ordinary school's advantages here? Can they really claim superiority over special schools where teaching is concerned? Two features of ordinary schools can be brought in evidence: their experience of mixed ability teaching; and the fact that 'normal' standards of achievement are expected. Teachers in ordinary schools are used to dealing with pupils with a wide range of abilities and selecting teaching approaches and materials appropriate to their individual requirements. What pupils with special needs require is, in some respects, just an extension of this. Moreover, the fact that teachers encounter a wide range of achievement levels means that they are more likely to have high expectations of their pupils and to stretch them academically.

Needless to say, these arguments are open to question. Contrary views could well be held and indeed are. Much so-called mixed ability teaching is nothing of the sort, being geared to some hypothetical 'middle' of the class and quite inappropriate to many pupils at both ends of the ability spectrum. Moreover, some teachers in ordinary schools have neither the willingness nor the expertise that they need in order to teach pupils with special needs effectively.

It is easy to see that this can degenerate into a sterile, 'our-team-is-better-than-yours' argument. The empirical information that would settle it decisively is simply not available. The debate is useful, though, in drawing attention to a core element of any teaching provision however organised. Good teaching skills are not so common or so easily acquired that they can be taken for granted. The concern of any school that would be effective must be to ensure that *its* staff have the requisite teaching skills, regardless of whether other schools have them or not.

Other considerations

What emerges from the foregoing is that there is no clear balance of advantage for or against integration. Whether we look at academic attainment, social development, or curricular range, the available evidence does not establish conclusively that pupils with special needs are better off in either special schools or ordinary schools. Moreover, the discussion has shown that because of the measurement and comparison problems it is extremely difficult to obtain convincing evidence. A similar picture will emerge from later chapters on the cost of provision and on parental preference.

In some ways this is a fortunate outcome, since it leaves the way clear for more fundamental concerns. It also eliminates the need to reconcile potential conflicts. It is possible, for instance, that considerations of academic attainment and cost could point in different directions. One could imagine a scenario where, if academic attainment was the predominant concern, ordinary schools were to be preferred, whereas if cost was the decisive factor the choice would have to be special schools. Were this to happen, it could be extremely difficult to decide between them since there is no self-evident priority amongst the different practical considerations.

There are two further sets of considerations to take into account when deciding on integration, both quite different from the empirical concerns raised so far. The first has to do with legislation. Increasingly around the world legislation is being enacted that seeks to minimise – and in a few cases eliminate – the role of the special school and to establish the ordinary school as the normal place of education for all pupils. Britain is no exception here. As detailed in chapter 3, a new Education Act relating to pupils with special educational needs was passed in 1981 and came into force two years later. One of the key requirements of the Act has to do with integration. Apart from certain specified exceptions, all children are to be educated in an ordinary school: the local authority is charged with making arrangements for pupils with special educational needs to attend ordinary schools, and the schools themselves must ensure that these pupils engage in the activities of the school alongside other pupils.

As we have seen, this Act has not led to rapid changes. It was well recognised that development had to be gradual: it was not a simple matter of transferring pupils from one location to another but of redirecting resources, setting up new administrative and other procedures, and engaging in major curriculum development – all in a context of system change. These changes must be achieved gradually, particularly if the undoubted strengths of the special school sector are not to be lost in the process. The Act has, however, totally redrawn the legislative context within which special education is provided, and conforming to it will undoubtedly lead to significant changes over the next few years. There is no equality of status between special schools and ordinary schools as far as the Act is concerned. The ordinary school is the normal place of education for all, and the special school can only be considered as a fall-back option when the ordinary school cannot make the requisite educational provision.

INTEGRATION AS A MORAL ISSUE

The final consideration is different from the others. They have all had to do with the accidentals of integration as it were. The prevailing legislation and how it is enforced could have been different. The empirical evidence on academic achievement and social development could have come down decisively one way or the other. Cost comparisons could have favoured one type of provision significantly more than another. Running beneath all of these – and determining what significance is to attach to them – is an ethical dimension. Integration is, in the end, a moral issue, revolving around the rights of individuals and society's willingness to acknowledge these rights in effective terms. There are three rights that concern us here: the right to education; the right to equality of educational opportunity; and the right to participate in society.

It is well to realise how recent is the acknowledgement of a universal right to education. Prior to 1971 a considerable number of people were formally deemed to be ineducable: they were regarded as being incapable of benefiting from education and so were not educated. In Great Britain at least, this is no longer the case and all children are accorded a formal right to education. It might be questioned how widely acknowledged by the general public this is – many people find it hard to credit that people with gross handicapping conditions can benefit from education and still see their institutional needs in terms of care rather than education – but that is another discussion. Acknowledging the right to education is not yet to accept integration but it is a step toward it: if children attend schools rather than junior training centres a major segregative barrier has been removed.

Equality of educational opportunity poses more difficult questions. Equality of opportunity is an important principle and carries a powerful emotive charge. It is quite general in its import however, and its practical implications can be difficult to establish. It does not, for instance, mean that all people should be treated the same. As far as education is concerned, equality of opportunity is not secured by equal educational treatment. Children are not equal and should not be treated as if they were. Indeed justice requires that they be treated unequally. This is widely recognised in practice – thus, a deaf pupil can receive possibly ten times the amount of educational resources that the average hearing pupil does.

What we need is a means of translating the general principle of equal opportunity into concrete rights that are meaningful at the level of actual educational provision. This is given by the notion of differential educational treatment. Since children are different from each other, they must be treated in different ways in order to reach common goals. This raises a host of practical questions as to how different forms of provision relate to agreed goals and what degree of difference in how children are treated is sustainable in practice. The detail of differential educational treatment has to be worked out in the individual case – there could be argument in the case of the deaf pupil above, for instance, as to whether the amount of resources should be ten times the average rather than eight times or twelve times. (For a more extended discussion of how differential educational treatment, in the context of ethnic minority provision, is justified, see Hegarty and Lucas, 1978.)

Once the principle of equality of educational opportunity accorded by differential educational treatment is established, it marks a further stage in the normalising of educational provision. Children with special needs have a right not merely to education but to an enhanced level of educational provision. Again, this does not enjoin integration but it does bring it still closer, since the enhancement provided must be defined to some extent in terms of a common educational system. Provision for these pupils is not a totally separate matter from mainstream provision, nor does it belong within an isolated enclave. It has to be conceived and delivered within a comprehensive framework that takes account of the normal educational provision made for all pupils. This requirement makes a significant step toward integration.

Finally, there is the right to participate in society. This is often expressed in negative terms – people should not be discriminated against or suffer restrictions over and above those common to other people. In aducation there is a common American term which speaks of educating children in the 'least restrictive environment'. These negative formulations abound because barriers and the absence of participation are more evident and easier to pin-point than actual participation. Positive statements describing people's participation in society tend to be general and unhelpfully vague.

As far as education is concerned, the right to participate in society means that children must not suffer needless restrictions in their access to education, in the range of curriculum on offer to them or in the quality of education they receive. It would be reasonable to argue that it also requires that children should not, without good cause, be educated separately from their age peers. Expressed positively, it means that children have the right to attend ordinary schools alongside age peers unless there are specific reasons to the contrary. More than that, they have the right to participate in the life of a school as well as just attend it. In order to specify what this means in practice it would be necessary to enumerate those aspects of the life of the school that are part of the common experience of pupils attending that school. Pupils with special needs have, then, the same right to participate in these aspects, and anything that prevents them from doing so is a denial of rights.

Between them, these three rights or principles – the right to education, the right to equality of educational opportunity and the right to participate in society – add up to a powerful case for integration. Accepting them means accepting that every child has the right to attend an ordinary school and to receive there an appropriate education delivered as part of the school's normal pattern of educational provision. It means, moreover, that the pragmatic considerations – academic attainment, cost, and so on – are of secondary inportance. They cannot be ignored: if, for instance, a given form of provision led consistently to inferior academic results no amount of recourse to basic principles could justify maintaining that form of provision. Likewise, the costs of making provision in different ways have to be taken into considera- tion. They must be kept in perspective however. In particular, if basic rights have to be set aside on pragmatic grounds it has to be clearly recognised what is happening. When a pupil is excluded from an ordinary school for reasons of cost, or difficulty of teaching, or whatever, this does not mean that the pupil does not have the same rights as other pupils but rather that we are failing to guarantee them. There may be good or bad reasons for doing so, but the fact remains that for this pupil basic rights are being set aside.

TOWARD A SYNTHESIS

A distinction was made at the beginning of this chapter between pupils with problems in learning already in ordinary schools and pupils currently in special schools. The arguments about integration are different for the two groups. Much of the chapter has been given over to outlining the different arguments. The considerations in the first case have to do with bringing about changes in ordinary schools and ensuring that certain types of educational provision are made. In the second case the concern has been with desegregation, and various practical considerations as well as matters of principle have been examined.

The two sets of considerations do converge in the end. Both are underpinned by a common concern for rights – all children are entitled to an appropriate education, delivered with a minimum of restriction and isolation from peers. Both point to a reform of schooling, through the creation of schools that provide within a single context differentiated education programmes to cater for the full range of pupils' educational needs. The next chapter gives an idea of what such schools look like. They will be different from most present-day schools in numerous respects. The requisite provision, for either group, cannot be made by simply attaching an extra component to an existing school, even though the use of such 'attachments' – in the form of special units and extra teachers – is very common. The changes needed cut right across the school. They affect the very core of its activities – what is taught, how pupils are grouped, the teaching and learning methods used, how staff are deployed. These are all interrelated, and changes affecting one element cannot be made in isolation from the others.

A final, practical consideration linking the two groups is that there is overlap between the types of provision they need. Making changes in a school so that it is better suited to one group will also make it more suited to the other group. This is particularly true of situations where schools seek to integrate pupils with significant problems in learning – the so-called two per cent. Teachers discover that these pupils cannot be taught effectively without very explicit attention to teaching approach. Skills of diagnostic assessment, programme planning, and monitoring of progress have to be brought into play. In practice, these skills frequently turn out to have clear relevance to other pupils as well. Teachers realise that they have not, perhaps, been doing a particularly good job with some pupils already in the school, and that the latter stand to benefit from the greater attention to individual learning needs and the careful matching of teaching approach to learning need that are taken for granted in the case of the two per cent.

Teachers may discover also that the two per cent are not totally different from pupils already at the school. Sometimes there is a clear continuum in terms of the pattern of learning difficulties. Even if this is not the case and individual pupils have quite special learning difficulties, as associated, for instance, with sensory impairment, the teaching they require still fits into the common pattern by which schools respond to special educational needs – identify the learning needs, devise an appropriate programme, implement it, and monitor progress. Seeing all pupils in this way leads to a perception of a common school where every pupil is special but none so extraordinary as to merit exclusion.

The elements of school reform

Integration is essentially about school reform. Major changes have to be made in ordinary schools if they are to cater adequately for pupils with special needs, whether these be pupils already at the school or pupils currently in a special school. What does this entail in practice? What kind of changes are necessary? What does a reformed school look like?

This chapter addresses these questions. It analyses the key elements of the ordinary school where reform is necessary. The curriculum is at the core of the process since the design and delivery of the curriculum provide the central definition of a school. Any curricular considerations must be set within the context of the school's academic organisation since this provides the framework within which the curriculum is delivered. Staffing must be considered also, since the kind of staff and the ways in which they are deployed determine as much as anything else what changes are possible. All of these topics are developed in detail in the different volumes of the series. The purpose of this chapter is to provide an overview and link the different elements of school reform together.

ACADEMIC ORGANISATION

If we start with the school's academic organisation – since this provides the framework within which teachers deliver the curriculum – a first set of changes becomes evident. Academic organisation is concerned in a major way with how pupils are grouped for teaching purposes. It has to do also with arrangements made for any specialist teaching and with the problems of timetable construction.

Pupil grouping

The groups in which pupils spend their school day provide the setting for both learning and social interaction. Possible groupings vary widely in British schools, particularly at secondary level. Chapter 7 outlines the variety of ways in which pupils with special needs can be grouped for teaching purposes; these range from placement in an ordinary class with little modification to existing arrangements to quite complicated link programmes spanning special schools and ordinary schools.

There are two key points about such groupings. Firstly, they must be such as to allow pupils to receive the special help they may require; and, secondly, they must allow all pupils to be real members of the school community. These requirements can sometimes pull in opposite directions. If teachers feel that particular pupils require such specialist provision that they must be dealt with quite differently from other pupils, these pupils may end up being segregated from their peers and not being members of the school community in any real sense. The extreme form of this occurs when a large group of pupils with special needs are taught separately and become a virtual special school within the confines of an ordinary school. (This situation, when it occurs, is particularly unfortunate since the group has neither the advantages of autonomous special school status nor the benefits of being in a mainstream setting.) It can also happen with smaller groups. Special classes are often set up for pupils perceived as having similar – and highly specialised – teaching needs. These classes are often based on the traditional categories of handicap – visual impairment, communication disorder, and so on. If the teaching needs of these pupils are conceived and provided for in a separate way from other pupils, segregation is again the almost inevitable result. They run the risk of being peripheral to the main academic work of the school and having a limited social participation in it.

Precisely how pupils are to be grouped will depend on local circumstances. The two principles of ensuring adequate provision and of facilitating participation will point to different prescriptions in different schools, and arrangements made for pupils with special needs must reflect how the school as a whole is structured. An NFER study of classroom arrangements found that mixed ability classes were widely perceived as advantageous in offering the flexibility of teaching approach necessary for teaching pupils with special needs (Hodgson, Clunies-Ross and Hegarty, 1984). When pupils are rigidly streamed, the group at the bottom is sharply defined, often acquiring thereby a negative and isolated status. Schools in the NFER study found it helpful if no more than two pupils with special needs were allocated to any one class in order to contain the demands made on the teacher. Furthermore, two pupils with similar special needs could be accommodated more easily than two pupils with very different needs.

Arrangements for supplementary teaching

Another aspect of academic organisation is the arrangements made for supplementary teaching provided *outside* mainstream lessons. This arises when pupils who have the capacity to benefit from regular attendance at mainstream lessons nevertheless need extra individual attention over and above what can be provided during the lessons. The supplementary teaching generally takes the form of equipping them with the concepts, knowledge, and skills that they require in order to take full part in mainstream lessons. These arrangements are related to pupil groupings, since they are relevant only when pupils are grouped for teaching purposes in certain ways. They are independent of pupil grouping, however, and represent a separate organisational strand.

The provision of supplementary teaching raises numerous organisational questions relating to lesson planning, room allocation, timetabling, staff deployment, and liaison arrangements. Close collaboration between support teacher and class teacher is particularly inportant. Both need a common understanding of the aims and content of lessons. The support teacher must gauge the support to the class teacher's lesson strategies as well as to the pupil's apparent need of support, and can also give useful feedback to the class teacher. The latter, in turn, must take account of the support that is being provided and gear lesson presentation accordingly, particularly if pupils regularly miss lessons in order to receive the support.

Hodgson et al. (1984) found that the schools in their study arranged supplementary teaching in a variety of ways, so as to come before lessons, during lessons, or after them.

Pre-lesson teaching

Specific instruction given before a lesson, usually on an individual basis, served the purpose of introducing new topics in advance, explaining potentially difficult vocabulary, and giving preliminary practice in skills that would be required. Good liaison was found to be particularly important. Support teachers needed adequate advance information on the content to be covered, along with copies of resource material as appropriate. There were examples in the schools studied of this information being provided on a regular weekly, monthly, or even half-termly basis. A major difficulty in practice was finding time to meet in order to exchange information, discuss pupils' progress and consider any problems arising.

Support provided during a lesson

When supplementary teaching was provided during a mainstream lesson this often took place in the classroom, either through team teaching or the use of a second adult in some way. Apart from exchanging information, it was important for the staff concerned to have good working relationships. There were differences in how this form of support was used as between primary and secondary schools. Younger pupils were taken aside for short spells of additional work, generally to use different resource materials from the rest of the class. At secondary level support often took the form of an alternative activity that called for supervision rather than support. Older pupils were more likely to take the initiative in removing themselves from the mainstream of a lesson when they judged it advantageous to do so.

Post-lesson teaching

The most common form of supplementary teaching was that which came after lessons. It necessarily had to be remedial rather than preventive in orientation. The support teacher relied on the pupils to supply information on their difficulties with the lesson. The usual pattern was to work with individual pupils – as soon as possible after a lesson – finding out what had been covered, responding to pupils' questions and generally making sure that the content was correctly and fully understood.

Pre- and post-lesson support

In a few schools supplementary teaching as outlined was provided before *and* after lessons in an integrated way. This constituted a powerful mix of preventive and remedial support and was especially valuable in areas where learning was sequential. By its very nature this form of support is intensive in terms both of staff contact time and of planning and consultation.

Timetabling

A school's timetable is the framework whereby different groups are taught a range of subjects, possibly at different levels, using common resources. The resources – teachers, curriculum material, classrooms, and laboratories – are necessarily finite, and often scarce. These have to be shared out according to some criteria, be they explicit or implicit. Particularly in secondary schools, which offer a wide range of subjects, this can entail complex arrangements and conflicting demands that can only be met by making compromises.

The timetable embodies these compromises and it offers a clear means of examining to what extent pupils with special needs are receiving equitable treatment. Is special teaching support provided on a normal timetabled basis, or does it have to be fitted in around the edges, when 'proper subjects' have been allocated, and made to depend upon staff availability? Do groups containing pupils with special needs have appropriate access to specialist rooms and laboratories and on the same basis as other groups? Do pupils with special needs have the same choice of option subjects as other pupils?

These questions are not easily answered. The demands on the timetable are generally such that the ideal situation is not possible for every pupil. Pupils with special needs must not be allowed to dictate the timetable. Equally, however, they must not always be the ones to miss out when compromises have to be made. What is necessary is that information on their learning difficulties and curriculum requirements is assembled and incorporated into timetable planning in a considered fashion. In this way, arrangements for them will take their place alongside arrangements made for other pupils, and both extremes will be avoided. This process is likely to add to the complexity of timetabling and necessitate even more compromises, but it is the only authentic way of proceeding if pupils with special needs are to be integral members of the school.

CURRICULUM RANGE

The school's academic organisation provides the framework within which its work is done. Whilst it is important to achieve the right framework, it is even more important to attend to what goes on within it. This fact puts the spotlight on what is taught to different groups of pupils.

We saw in the previous chapter how the relative merits of special schools and ordinary schools are sometimes debated in terms of breadth of curriculum. However that debate is settled, it is generally acknowledged that the wider curriculum of the ordinary school is not adequately available to pupils with special needs. When pupils spend the bulk of their time doing basic work in language and number, when teachers in specialist subjects such as science or music do not taken them seriously for teaching purposes, when whole areas of the mainstream curriculum remain closed to them, then there is cause for concern. Not only are pupils' educational needs not being met, not only are they probably worse off in curricular terms than if they were in a special school with a narrow range of subjects, but the necessary reform of the ordinary school has not even begun.

If a school is really to open its doors to pupils with special needs – moving beyond locational integration – there is need of considerable curriculum development. This means modifying what is taught and how it is taught. It means establishing a broad curriculum framework that can encompass the diverse needs of pupils with exceptional talents and those who learn most things with difficulty. Here again the tension between 'normalisation' and special provision is evident. Ensuring a wider curricular experience for all pupils may appear to conflict with responding to particular needs, interests, or talents. The goal of the school reform in view is to have schools where these conflicts are resolved within a curriculum framework that is relevant and differentiated as well as broad.

The HMI document on the curriculum from 5 to 16 (DES, 1985a) offers a comprehensive curriculum framework that is pertinent here. It is addressed to schools in general and does not single out special needs. It is no less relevant for that however: if anything, it is the more relevant since special needs are located *within* a context rather than themselves being the context. By a nice irony indeed the document takes its statement of the goals of education from the Warnock Report:

> to enlarge a child's knowledge, experience and imaginative under-standing and thus his awareness of moral values and capacity for enjoyment; and secondly to enable him to enter the world after formal education is over as an active participant in society and a responsible contributor to it ...

It also repeats the Warnock observation that for some children 'the road they have to travel towards the goals is smooth and easy, for others it is fraught with obstacles'. It goes on to affirm that the goals apply to all children and that there must be a unity of purpose across the age range and throughout the school system (paras 6 and 7).

The document regards a school's curriculum as 'all those activities designed or encouraged within its organisational framework to promote the intellectual, personal, social and physical develop-ment of its pupils' (para 11). In addition to formal lessons, it includes 'so-called extracurricular activities as well as those features which produce the school's "ethos", such as the quality of relationships, the concern for equality of opportunity' and the values embedded in the day-to-day life of the school. Pupils learn from all of these things, so it is important that they form a coherent whole along with lesson content and the other formal aspects of school life.

Five desirable characteristics of a comprehensive curriculum are outlined: breadth, balance, relevance, differentiation, and progres-sion and continuity. The curriculum should be broad in the sense of bringing all pupils into contact with an agreed range of areas of learning and experience. It should be balanced in that it allows the adequate development of each area without undue specialisation or the neglect of any area. It should be relevant to pupils' present and likely future needs, and be seen as such by pupils, their parents, and the wider society. It must be sufficiently differentiated to allow for differences in pupils' abilities and situations. Finally, the curriculum must take account of the fact that children's development is a continuous process and provide for a systematic progression from one learning stage to the next.

As to what should go into the curriculum framework, the document proposes two organising principles: areas of learning and experience; and elements of learning. These provide complement-ary and intersecting perspectives. Between them they facilitate a powerful synthesis of the range of curricular activity in schools and point the way toward planned reform.

Areas of learning and experience are the broad lines of develop-ment that should feature in a rounded education. (These are what writers in the philosophy of education refer to as 'the forms of knowledge'.) The document proposes nine areas:

- aesthetic and creative
- human and social
- linguistic and literary
- mathematical
- moral
- physical
- scientific
- spiritual
- technological.

All pupils have an entitlement in each of these areas, and every school should ensure that each is adequately represented in the work of pupils.

The different areas are not discrete, nor do pupils have to engage in them separately. Particularly where younger children are concerned, there are numerous possibilities for single activities to contribute to several areas of learning. Thus, cooking can involve creative, social, linguistic, mathematical, scientific, and technologi-cal learning. Schools can examine existing practice to ascertain the extent to which the different areas are covered and decide on any changes or additions that may be required.

The elements of learning are fourfold: knowledge, concepts, skills, and attitudes. They intersect with the areas of learning and experience in that the elements are acquired in the context of the areas. Thus, there are knowledge, concepts, skills, and attitudes associated with the mathematical area that are distinctive, and different from the knowledge, etc. associated with the human and social area. These elements can be subdivided in various ways to facilitate the process of curriculum design.

The curriculum framework set out by the HMI document is an extremely general one, valuable for its coherence and comprehen-siveness and likely to secure widespread assent. It should also achieve its target of providing schools with useful checklists in examining their curricular offerings and making changes to them. The very generality, however, means that it has little to offer on actual curriculum design. The document is silent on how to move from the abstract principles underlying the framework to the specific decisions that schools have to take on what pupils are to be taught and how in practice they should be taught. Nor does it take account of the widely disparate situations in which schools find themselves as regards curriculum planning. It is seldom that a school can start with a clean sheet: existing staff, resources, procedures, and school organisation are inescapable parts of the context within which any curriculum reform will be conducted and they may set considerable restrictions on what is possible.

A notable example of an effort to translate a general curriculum framework into detailed prescriptions for actual schools is the Inner London Education Authority (ILEA) report *Improving Secondary Schools* (ILEA, 1984). There should be no doubt as to the significance of this document. ILEA may be a single local authority but it is a very large one (population two-and-a-quarter million) and faces an exceptional range of social and educational problems. Moreover, the authority has signalled a clear intention of implementing the recommendations of the report. (It may be worth noting that David Hargreaves who chaired the Committee that produced the report was subsequently appointed Chief Inspector with ILEA – a post which has considerable influence on the shape of the curriculum in the authority's schools.)

Improving Secondary Schools predated the 1985 HMI document but it took account of earlier HMI and DES curriculum documents that presaged it. It accepts the broad outlines of the HMI framework, particularly the concern to move away from within-department curriculum planning based on separate subjects to a whole-school approach based on more broadly conceived areas of experience. It acknowledges the difficulty of doing this in view of the relative autonomy of subject departments in schools and the grip of the examination system on the curriculum. The report does point to successful examples of whole-curriculum planning in ILEA schools however. It also draws on principles of curriculum planning developed by the ILEA inspectorate.

This leads to a detailed set of proposals for the fourth and fifth year curriculum. (It is here that the separate subjects are most isolated from each other and also where the greatest divergence of practice between schools occurs.) There should be a common curriculum taking up between 60 and 70 per cent of pupils' time. This would have six elements:

1. English language and literature.
2. Mathematics.
3. Science.
4. Personal and social education, and religious education.
5. At least one 'aesthetic' subject.
6. At least one 'technical' subject.

The remainder, covering about one-third of the school week, would be for either additional periods in compulsory subjects or for free options. Pupils would choose from: classical and modern languages, history, geography, economics, commercial and business studies, physical education, additional science subjects, additional technical subjects, additional English and mathematics.

What gives these proposals bite, and points up their relevance to pupils who are marginalised by the curricular organisation of many schools, is the emphasis on what pupils will experience as a result of them. What matters to pupils is not curriculum content *per se* but the curriculum-as-taught. The cornerstones for implementation here are: an insistence on active learning roles for pupils; and a proposal to break courses into shorter learning (and assessment) units.

It is an integral part of the proposals that pupils should be actively engaged in learning. The passive reception of knowledge is rejected as a major aim of schooling. Not only does it guarantee under-achievement and disaffection on the part of many pupils but it is fundamentally misguided in its emphasis. It is linked with the traditional polarisation between academic knowledge and practical skill, which is seen to be simplistic and misleading. In challenging the 'residual contempt' for practical activities prevalent within the education system, the report calls for more attention to skill acquisition, oral work, problem solving, and the application of learning to practical situations. This is not to elevate the practical to a higher status than the theoretical. It is, rather, to see the relationship between them in a new light. Dealing with life situations of any complexity calls for a fusion of theoretical and practical responses, and school curricula are irrelevant to the extent that they fail to take account of this.

The outcome of pupils engaging actively in a broadly conceived curriculum is that a wider set of achievements is recognised. The traditional academic curriculum, with its written exam orientation, is built around the capacity to organise propositional knowledge and especially to handle it in written form. Under this scheme other forms of achievement are seen as subsidiary, if not totally ignored. The ILEA document specifically draws attention to three other aspects of achievement:

1. The capacity to apply knowledge – practical and oral skills, investigation, problem solving.
2. Personal and social skills – communication, teamwork, initiative, leadership.
3. Motivation and commitment, perseverance in the face of difficulty.

This is not a hard-and-fast analysis of pupils' school achievement. Indeed, it differs slightly from the breakdown offered by Hargreaves in his book on the comprehensive school, where he proposed five sets of skills that schools should take into account: cognitive–intellectual; aesthetic–artistic; affective–emotive; physical–manual; and personal–social (Hargreaves, 1982). It offers an adequate schema for present purposes, however, and it will be a significant step forward if schools give due recognition to achievement in each of these areas.

The document contains a radical proposal for organising and assessing what is taught, which again has major implications for pupil involvement. In essence, this is to break courses down into shorter, more manageable units.

> Instead of setting out on a vague two-year educational journey towards nebulous and distant goals pupils should from the beginning of the fourth year embark on a series of six to eight week learning units, each of which has a more readily defined and perceived purpose, content and method of recording.

This would lead to '11 or 12 interconnected units, each of which is meaningful in itself and adapted to the time perspective of 14 year olds' (3.11.10). Whilst this would require major changes in how the curriculum is conceived, it is seen to offer significant advantages in motivating pupils, in gearing new work to what they have already mastered and in building up profiles of achievement.

ILEA has not been alone in its attempt to achieve practical school reform. The growing awareness that schools were not providing adequately for many pupils has led to numerous efforts to devise alternative programmes of work. These are generally not whole-school curricula since they are confined to a section of the school. Many are based on whole-curriculum planning however, and organise programmes that cut across the traditional subject boundaries.

The most notable activity in this context is the Lower Attaining Pupils' Programme. This is a national initiative running in 17 local education authorities and supported by central government funding from 1983 to 1987. The aim of the programme is 'to find ways of providing a more effective education for those pupils in their fourth and fifth year of secondary schooling for whom the current … system of public examinations was not designed' (DES, 1986b). It is worth noting that the Programme is subject to the most detailed scrutiny and analysis: each project has a local evaluation built into it; HMI have adopted a monitoring role and have published a report (HMI, 1986); and a team based at NFER is conducting a national evaluation on the Programme as a whole.

The initial guidelines to authorities were quite general. They indicated areas of work that might be included such as communication skills and profiling, but they did not lay down a curriculum framework to be implemented nor did they instruct authorities on the form their projects should take. The result has been a great diversity of project styles and approaches. In one authority it is confined to a single school whilst in another all the authority's secondary schools are involved. Some schools have a clearly defined group of pupils who spend most of the week together doing work devised specifically for them whilst others see the project as a development of its existing curriculum and involve the whole year group in aspects of it. A few schools have used the project as an opportunity to question the whole fourth/fifth year curriculum structure (Weston, 1986). The areas covered in the different projects range from pre-vocational skills to oral work, from residential activities to work experience, from establishing pupil profiles to fostering links with the local community.

Despite the diversity, some common strands of key significance are emerging. Weston points to 'a growing consensus about the importance of the *process* of learning, and the need to make this more explicit to learners and teachers'. This is exemplified by the emphasis on providing an active involvement in learning. Many projects

> try to involve pupils in a planning/decision-making sequence: defining the question or problem, generating alternative solutions, evaluating them and reaching a decision, planning and executing the preferred solution, reporting on this and reviewing the performance.

Whilst information on the outcomes of the Lower Attaining Pupils' Programme is still tentative, it is tackling major issues head on and could be a catalyst for significant curriculum reform. There is the bonus of being subject to comprehensive internal and external evaluation. The reflection and analysis generated by this should ensure that the lessons to be learnt from the Programme will be learnt and that the insights garnered and achievements made in particular schools and authorities will become available to other schools as well.

STAFFING

The curriculum is delivered by the school staff, and any curriculum reform has major implications for staffing. It goes without saying that an effective school will have an adequate number of staff with appropriate expertise and that these staff will be deployed in a planned but flexible way geared to the actual needs of pupils on roll. This is true for any area of the curriculum, be it mathematics, or art, or whatever.

Provision for special needs raises particular problems in this regard. It is not dealing with a straightforward curriculum area like the conventional school subjects, and the requisite expertise is neither as clearly defined nor as readily deployed. The expertise that teachers need cuts across the curriculum. They may need to know some facts about different disabilities and how they affect learning, but their principal expertise is pedagogical. They must be able, in different curriculum areas, to identify pupils' learning difficulties, devise practical ways of enhancing their learning and establish detailed procedures for monitoring their progress. It is the task of training, both initial and inservice, to ensure that the necessary expertise is acquired. This is discussed below in chapter 10.

Assuming that the training needs have been identified and are being met, we have to consider how the resultant expertise is to be deployed. How does the education that pupils receive benefit from the training given to their teachers? To examine this, we need to look at the distribution of expertise within schools, the range of tasks that specialist teachers can carry out, and the status accorded within schools to staff associated with special needs work.

Distribution of expertise

How is the requisite expertise to be distributed? Should it be concentrated in a small number of well-trained specialists or should it be spread across the entire school staff? The answers here will depend on the pattern of academic organisation within the school and, to a lesser extent, on the range of special needs. What is feasible, and advantageous, in a primary school with open-plan teaching will be different from the arrangements that might be made in a highly structured secondary school.

The exact relationship between the nature of pupils' special needs and the kind of teaching expertise required to meet them is the subject of controversy. Particular teaching approaches have been associated with the different categories of handicap. Now that the basis of the categories has been discredited in pedagogical terms, the matching of teaching approach to special need is no longer seen to be automatic or easy. The concern here is with the ways in which expertise is deployed rather than with the nature of the expertise itself. It has been assumed too readily in the past that certain types of impairment require particular concentrations of expertise. Visually impaired pupils in ordinary schools, for instance, have usually been grouped into special classes run by teachers with specialist training in visual impairment, and their presence in the school barely impinged on the other teachers. It takes the startling example of a school that disperses all its blind and partially sighted pupils throughout the classes, making their class teacher responsible for their teaching, to show that the traditional arrangement is not necessitated by teaching requirements.

The NFER study referred to earlier found that when schools made changes in their staffing establishment to take account of the presence of pupils with special needs, the changes fell into four broad categories:

1. *Employing specialist teacher(s)*. This is the most obvious way perhaps. One or more teachers with specialist training and experience in special needs are appointed to take responsibility for this area of work in the school. They co-ordinate the teaching of pupils with special needs and provide specific guidance for other staff. Where there is a sizeable number of such staff, as in some secondary schools, they may constitute a 'special needs' department comparable with the main subject departments in the school.

2. *Increasing the staffing complement of the school in a general way*. This is an alternative approach favoured by a small number of schools. It entails deploying the extra staff across the school as a whole so as to reduce class size and increase flexibility within the timetable. These staff may provide specific assistance with individual pupils but the principal responsibility for all pupils remains with class teachers. Indeed, some head teachers regard the latter as an essential characteristic of a truly comprehensive school and view the emergence of large special needs departments with disquiet: such departments allow class teachers to disclaim responsibility for pupils with special needs and are ultimately segregative.

3. *Extending the role of mainstream staff*. This is an inevitable feature of any arrangements that place pupils with special needs in mainstream lessons, since they make new teaching demands on the class teacher. In some cases, however, it is the only change since no extra staffing or other support is available. This can impose considerable demands on staff. It is a viable arrangement only if existing staff have the knowledge and confidence to teach these pupils or if adequate inservice training is provided.

4. *Increasing the allocation of ancillary staff*. The potential contribution of classroom assistants and other ancillary staff is too often neglected. Some schools enhance their educational provision by effective deployment of ancillary staff. They can free teachers to concentrate on teaching by reducing demands of a non-teaching nature. They can also engage in direct educational activities if given appropriate guidance and supervision.

Making use of specialist teachers

If a school is serious about provision for special needs, it will certainly want to have on its staff one or more teachers who are expert in the area. There are numerous tasks for such teachers to carry out. Firstly, they have to teach! However well-disposed and expert the main teacher body, it is likely that some teaching will have to be done by specialists in special needs. This is particularly so in the case of pupils with severe and complex learning difficulties and those who have a hearing impairment or other serious communication disorder. Sometimes, this teaching is so structured and intensive in nature that it is best provided on a one-to-one basis or in a small group withdrawn from the main class for a time. Pupils with emotional and behavioural difficulties often need such withdrawal. In all of these cases there is need of specialist teachers who have the requisite expertise and are timetabled appropriately.

Secondly, any teaching carried out must be underpinned by appropriate assessment, programme planning, and monitoring of progress. The skills required to carry out these interrelated tasks are part of the basic repertoire of any teacher. Pupils with special needs pose particular challenges however, and the skills may need to be developed to a far greater extent. It may be necessary, for instance, to use specialised assessment instruments. Drawing up an individual programme of work may benefit from prior experience of pupils who have similar problems and of using relevant curriculum materials.

Thirdly, specialist teachers have a major role to play in supporting colleagues. This is all the more important when pupils with special needs are spread around the school and made the responsibility of individual class teachers. It can take various forms: educating teachers on curriculum materials and teaching strategies; withdrawing individual pupils for supplementary work; joining a mainstream class in order to provide support in the course of a lesson; disseminating relevant information on pupils' handicapping conditions and how they affect learning, as well as drawing attention to significant changes as they occur; and promoting colleagues' professional development either directly themselves or by arranging inservice activities.

Finally, there are administrative tasks that may need to be carried out by a specialist teacher, certainly by somebody who has an overview of the situation of the pupils with special needs and is familiar with relevant local services. Central amongst such tasks is liaising with colleagues in external agencies – psychologists, speech therapists, physiotherapists, social workers, careers officers – in formulating programmes of work, reviewing progress and planning for the future. Time has to be spent in dealing with routine correspondence, arranging visits outside the school, receiving visitors, maintaining specialist equipment in good working order, and possibly administering drugs and checking hospital appointments. In some schools pupils with special needs are timetabled individually and the specialist teacher has to devise a range of timetables separately from the main school timetable.

Status of special needs work

Special needs work has not traditionally enjoyed high status in ordinary schools. Status tends to be associated with the perceived intellectual demands of a subject or area of work and with certain associated values. The top of the pile has at different times been classics, mathematics, and science. Working with less able pupils, so-called remedial teaching, has generally come near the bottom. The 'remedial pupils/remedial teacher' may have been a caricature but it did reflect a widespread perception. This perception is changing with the growing realisation that teaching simple concepts and skills to pupils with learning difficulties can be no less demanding pedagogically *and* intellectually than teaching complex matters to academically able pupils. Indeed, motivating the former group and ensuring that they actually learn can call for far greater teaching skills than instructing able, highly motivated pupils; the latter will learn a good deal even if the teaching is bad, whereas the former certainly will not.

Why is the status assigned to special needs staff important? Does it make a difference, other than helping the people concerned to feel good about their work? This latter is important, since it has implications for recruiting the right staff and motivating them for their work. If a job attracts no status and low rewards, it will be more difficult to recruit the most able people, and those who are recruited will not benefit from the motivation supplied by doing a socially esteemed job.

There is rather more to it than this however. If the staff have low status then so will the work. This can have debilitating implications. The worst of these is probably that the work will be hived off into a self-contained enclave. Mainstream staff will not see it as their concern and, if they do accept pupils with special needs in their classes, tend not to take them seriously for teaching purposes. Provision for special needs will not be integrated with the other work of the school, and the pupils concerned are likely to be offered a narrow curriculum. Moreover, the low status attached to the work can rub off on the pupils: their status as less able (or retarded, or dim, or worse) is confirmed and reinforced, and the resultant damage to their self-concepts makes learning even more difficult for them. Finally, there is the likelihood that the work will be under-resourced – in terms of staff and material but also as regards access to the timetable. The important areas of work are given priority in drawing up the timetable and less important, low status work is slotted in around these.

What can schools do to make sure that special needs work is given due status? A number of concrete steps can be taken:

- appoint staff at appropriate levels of seniority and build in opportunities for promotion
- recognise the specific expertise of these staff by utilising them in the school's arrangements for inservice work and for inducting new staff
- acknowledge their broader professional competence by involving them in the general life of the school, appointing them to appropriate committees and so on.

Hegarty and Pocklington (1982) cite an example that illustrates several of these pointers. This was the case of a teacher in charge of a special class in a primary school who was given responsibility for language development across the school; she maintained an overview of the language work in each class, advised colleagues on language materials and gave assistance with particular children who presented difficulties. Other schools can be cited that capitalise on particular talents or experience on the part of special needs teachers, such as music or physical education, in order to provide a richer curriculum for all pupils. There are numerous possibilities in secondary schools. Some schools that have a number of staff engaged in special needs work appoint a head of department on the same level (scale 4 or even Senior Teacher) as the other major departments in the school. This person may well be integrated into the management structure and curriculum planning activities of the school. Some schools require all teachers engaged in special needs work to do some mainstream teaching as well, to further their professional development and to demonstrate that they can contribute to the mainstream work of the school. These various tactics help to enhance the status of special needs teachers, by dispelling the myth that they are somehow substandard teachers and showing that, in fact, they need all the pedagogical skills of mainstream teachers – plus a great deal more besides.

This chapter has sought to delineate the characteristics of primary and secondary schools in which pupils with special needs are full members of the school community and receive an appropriate education there. In essence, the task has been to describe the 'new' comprehensive school which really is open to any pupil in the neighbourhood. This entails wide-ranging changes for many schools, since their curriculum, organisation and resourcing are based on excluding those pupils who present the greatest challenges.

The focus here has been on the curriculum. Academic organisation – pupil grouping, arrangements for supplementary teaching and timetabling – was considered first since this provides the structure within which the curriculum is delivered. Most of the chapter was given over to a discussion of curriculum frameworks which was not specific to pupils with special needs – necessarily so if a whole-school perspective is to be achieved. As well as outlining the characteristics of a comprehensive curriculum framework, it described some major implementation initiatives. Finally, the staffing implications of offering a new kind of curriculum were examined.

—7—
Pupil grouping

The way in which pupils are grouped for teaching purposes reflects the school's academic structure and is one of the most visible signs of how pupils fit into a school. It can also have a considerable bearing on the extent to which they participate in the life of the school. The previous chapter flagged this as an area of potential reform where pupils with special needs are concerned. The purpose of the present chapter is to describe the range of pupil groupings that are found in practice.

Provision for these pupils is often outlined in terms of a rough continuum from full integration into an ordinary class at one end to the relative segregation of placement in a special school at the other, with various intermediate arrangements where specialist resources are provided for differently composed groups of pupils with special needs. For present purposes the following listing will be used:

1. Pupils with special needs fitted into existing arrangements.
2. Mainstream placement with specialist support provided within the class.
3. Mainstream placement and withdrawal for specialist work.
4. Mainstream placement, attending special centre part-time.
5. Special centre placement, attending mainstream class part-time.
6. Special centre full-time.
7. Special school part-time, ordinary school part-time.

It should be stressed that any such listing is a relatively arbitrary way of dividing up a complex reality. The different groupings are not totally separate from each other: they overlap in practice, and provision in a given school can comprise elements of several different groupings. Also, one can only speak of a continuum in a relative and fairly imprecise sense. Depending on what aspect of the provision is being looked at – amount of individual teaching support, time spent with peers, departure from mainstream curriculum – it could be placed at different points along the continuum. For example, a pupil who is based in the mainstream might spend a substantial part of the day withdrawn for specialist teaching, whilst another who is based in a unit could well be attending a majority of mainstream lessons. What the listing does provide is a convenient, shorthand method of categorising the different ways in which ordinary schools group pupils with special needs and absorb them into their academic structures.

Pupils with special needs fitted into existing arrangements

This is the least intrusive arrangement at one level though, paradoxically, one that requires some of the most far-reaching changes in the school. Pupils with special needs are allocated to classes on the same basis – of age, alphabetical order, etc. – as other pupils, and all teachers are responsible for any pupils with special needs they happen to have in their classes. This is how schools have traditionally disposed the so-called '18 per cent'. It can be adopted also as the way of teaching pupils with more pronounced difficulties, though this is relatively uncommon.

A particular advantage of this arrangement is that it avoids formalising the distinction between pupils with special needs and the others. There are differences between them, of course, but they are neither as clear cut nor as fixed as the institutionalised labelling associated with other arrangements implies. It also facilitates a recognition of the fact that those pupils designated as having special needs are not the only ones that need extra help in their learning. In any class there will be pupils who do not stand out as having significant learning difficulties but who have difficulties none the less and who are likely to benefit from some specialist teaching.

The drawback of this arrangement is obvious: it requires that all teachers be competent to teach pupils who have special educational needs. This is a tall order, and one that represents a considerable challenge for many schools and teachers. It calls for a major programme of inservice training which without turning every teacher into a specialist will equip them to cater for a wide range of special needs in their class. It also calls for other changes in the school – smaller classes, increased ancillary back-up, high levels of curriculum resourcing, good systems for record keeping and for communication between staff. When every teacher is responsible for all the pupils with special needs in their class, the specialist resources that might in other arrangements be concentrated in a special needs department must be available in a dispersed form throughout the school.

This model of special needs provision is, in some ways, a limiting case. Its greatest use perhaps is in highlighting a direction in which a school's arrangements can move and in counteracting the strong trend toward centralising provision and responsibility for pupils with special needs. There will always be pupils whose learning

difficulties are so great that no class teacher in an ordinary school
,could be expected to cope unaided. What this model does is to
demonstrate that the number of such pupils can and should be
reduced and that it is possible for class teachers to have greater
teaching responsibility for all pupils in the class.

Mainstream placement with specialist support provided within the class

Pupils with special needs belong to the school's normal classes,
usually at the local school, and receive all their teaching in them.
They are not necessarily the sole responsibility of the class teacher,
since specialist support of various kinds is available. The resources
for support are decentralised and brought to the pupil and the class
teacher instead of being concentrated in one place so that pupils
with special needs have to come to them. The requisite support can
take various forms depending on the particular needs of the
individual. In the case of a physically handicapped pupil it can be
the presence of an ancillary helper plus visits from a physiotherapist; for a pupil with impaired hearing or vision it can mean regular
input from a school-based specialist teacher or a peripatetic advisory
teacher; a pupil with speech or language problems may be visited by
a speech therapist; a teacher with specific responsibility for special
needs may help out in the case of pupils with generalised learning
difficulties.

These different staff will work in a variety of ways. The ancillary
worker will attend to pupils' care needs, sometimes outside the
classroom as necessary, but may have an instructional function as
well. This can range from supervising mobility activities or
implementing a programme of exercises drawn up by a physiotherapist, to working in the classroom to instruction from the teacher or
speech therapist. Visiting staff have the option of working directly
with pupils or concentrating on the teacher or ancillary. In the
former case, they will carry out assessments, teach or give specific
therapy; in the latter, they will instruct staff and equip them to deal
more effectively with the pupils in their charge.

In some cases a school will designate a teacher as responsible for
special needs. This role can be particularly advantageous here. The
designated teacher can carry out a wide range of functions that
facilitate the smooth running of this form of provision: conduct or
assist in conducting assessments: provide direct teaching support
when in class; advise on teaching approaches; allocate ancillary staff
and monitor their working; acquire specialist equipment and
resources, and supervise their use and maintenance; assist in record
keeping and ensure that appropriate information is passed on from

teacher to teacher; liaise with external agencies and co-ordinate the work of any external specialists.

Mainstream placement and withdrawal for specialist work

Pupils with special needs belong to the school's normal classes and receive most of their teaching in them but they are withdrawn for some specialist work, e.g., teaching, auditory training, specific therapies. This can be provided by a member of the school staff, possibly a designated special needs teacher, or by a peripatetic specialist. The essential difference between this arrangement and the previous one is in the location of the resources being utilised: in the previous case the resources are brought to the pupil, whereas here the pupil must leave peers from time to time in order to go to the resources.

This form of provision is shaped very much by how the support is provided. On the one hand, it can come out of the school's own resources, either from individual staff or from a 'resource' area; on the other, it can come from peripatetic staff – usually teachers or therapists. The resource model, though relatively uncommon in this country, is well regarded elsewhere as a means of providing special education. It has particular advantages when there are a number of pupils on roll who have similar special educational needs.

The resource model entails a concentration of specialist equipment and materials into a single area of the school where staff can come and see what is available, receive advice on what to use, and arrange to borrow what they need. It is also a place where individual or small group work can be conducted when pupils are withdrawn from mainstream lessons. There are particular advantages in the case of visually impaired pupils when bulky equipment, such as closed circuit television, is not easily transported around the school, or when individuals need a quiet area to practise braille typing.

The other main input to withdrawal work is from peripatetic staff – advisory teachers, often with specific expertise in hearing or visual impairment, speech therapists and physiotherapists. They will be needed when schools do not have the requisite expertise in-house. This is most likely to arise when there are pupils on roll whose learning is particularly problematic or when there are pupils with a diversity of special educational needs that call for a corresponding range of expertise. Peripatetic input is an obvious way of giving them access to the necessary expertise. In some cases it is the only feasible means of doing so. Speech therapists, for instance, are in short supply and those who work in the school sector have to divide their time between many schools.

There can be pitfalls in relying on external staff. If a school has no designated special needs teacher on its own staff and special needs provision comes mainly from peripatetic input, there may be problems of management and liaison. The visiting staff are answerable to their own head of service, not to the school head, and whilst this is not necessarily a bad thing it does mean that the school management has no responsibility for significant activities going on within the school. When there are differences of opinion, the split in responsibility may well exacerbate the situation. Liaison is a concern at two levels – simply ensuring that pupils are available when peripatetic staff come and that the withdrawal arrangements are as little disruptive as possible, and passing on information to school staff. The latter is often a problem and school staff complain that there is no time for discussion or for visiting staff to explain what they are doing, suggest how their work might dovetail with class work, and offer general advice on teaching strategies.

Mainstream placement, attending special centre part-time

By 'special centre' here is meant a special class or unit – the difference is largely one of size – where pupils with special needs are taught separately from their peers. Under this arrangement pupils register and receive some teaching in mainstream groups but they also spend some of their teaching time in a segregated special centre. The teaching in a special centre can be based on particular aspects of the curriculum, the same for all pupils in the centre, or it can be geared to providing flexible programmes for individual pupils.

In primary schools the special centre is usually a single class run by the teacher responsible for special needs. In secondary schools it can be a fully-fledged department of the school, comparable in size and staffing to the main subject departments. The special centre is usually housed in its own room or suite of rooms, which can be purpose built or converted from spare classrooms. (Some schools manage to have the special centre in the main body of the school whereas others relegate them to the periphery, possibly in substandard huts; this latter situation is unfortunate since, apart from the difficulties of physical access, it tends to imply that the special centre is marginal to the real work of the school.) The special centre normally carries out the functions of the resource area as described above, so that care staff and other ancillaries are based there and any input from peripatetic specialists will be arranged through it.

The curriculum offerings of special centres vary greatly – in accordance with school philosophy, the learning needs of the pupils involved, and the length of time for which they are withdrawn. The predominant emphasis is on language and, to a lesser extent, number. Some staff believe that it is so important to build up skills in these areas that pupils are withdrawn from mainstream classes in English and mathematics to follow tailor-made programmes in the special centre. Alternatively, pupils may drop one or more mainstream subjects in order to provide time to supplement mainstream English lessons with further work on language. This tends to occur, for example, with secondary-age hearing impaired pupils who drop foreign languages in order to work on English or receive language-oriented assistance with other subjects. A potential weakness of this model, where pupils work on the basics of language and number in a special centre and attend mainstream lessons for selected other subjects, is that mainstream staff see them as the responsibility of special centre staff and do not take them seriously for teaching purposes in their own lessons. This may mean that, while pupils are attending science and geography lessons and are taught by subject specialists, they may not be benefiting as they should because the subject matter is not being presented in ways that are appropriate to them.

If a special centre is committed to flexibility, it will have to devise a variety of ways for dealing with individual pupils. Some of these will be identical to the withdrawal model described above where pupils leave mainstream lessons on an individual basis for specific work sessions. These and related approaches depend on analysing pupils' curriculum difficulties and devising means of meeting them. If pupils have difficulties of initial comprehension in a subject area, it may be necessary to work through topics before they are introduced to the class as a whole; this makes it possible to anchor a topic by means of pertinent examples, explain potentially difficult vocabulary, and work on any necessary skills. Alternatively, the preferred approach may be supplementary teaching that comes after mainstream lessons. Here the pupils themselves will often point to the difficulties they have had – something that is generally easier for them to do in a subsequent small group than in the course of a mainstream lesson – and the teacher then works through the content of the lesson, checking what has been understood, answering any questions, and relating the subject matter to the pupils' level of comprehension.

Preparing pupils for adult life is often a major concern of special centres in secondary schools. This is an area of work where special schools have been particularly active in recent years and some have built up highly effective leavers' programmes. As a result, staff responsible for special needs in ordinary schools face pressure to ensure that pupils do not miss out on the preparation for adult life that they would receive in a good special school. There may be some mainstream provision they can draw upon, but at best this is insufficient on its own and must be supplemented and at worst is irrelevant to pupils with special needs. In either case it is likely that special centres will wish to develop specific work on social and life skills – body care and presentation, transport and mobility, personal relationships, domestic skills, money management, dealing with institutions, and so on. Some special centres organise work experience separately from any mainstream arrangements because there has to be far greater involvement of staff in setting up and monitoring placements. Likewise, careers education and guidance may be provided separately in order to take account of the narrower range of choices generally available to pupils with special needs.

Special centre placement, attending mainstream class part-time

Pupils are based in a special centre and receive much of their teaching there but spend some time in mainstream classes as well. The way in which time is apportioned can vary, but the amount of time spent in the centre is usually considerable. This form of organisation is regularly used for hearing impaired pupils and those who have moderate learning difficulties.

In many respects this arrangement is identical to the previous one: staff complement and deployment, pupils' timetables and how their time is divided between the centre and mainstream lessons, the physical location of the centre – all may well be the same in both cases. The critical difference is in the lines of responsibility for pupils and the resulting implications. When pupils are based in a special class or unit as distinct from a normal class or tutor group, they are likely to be perceived – by peers, by staff, and by themselves – as different. Their form tutor is a 'special' teacher, their form registration group is a specially selected one, and they stand in a somewhat distant relationship to the rest of the school. When all of this is added to the fact that much of their teaching is arranged separately from peers, the net effect is to reinforce their isolation and their singular status.

On the positive side, it is argued that this sort of arrangement makes it easier to secure resources for them and ensure that the available resources are used to best effect. In some cases extra staff are assigned to a school on the basis of the number of pupils registered in the special centre, and if the emphasis was switched to mainstream placements it would be more difficult to obtain the same staffing resources. Likewise, capitation payments may be higher in the case of pupils registered in a special centre, so that the school has a pecuniary motivation! As regards deploying the resources and monitoring pupils' programmes of work, there are certain advantages in having a centralised responsibility for pupils with special needs. Specialist staff are often best placed to maintain an overview of their work. Apart from having a better understanding of their learning needs, they should also be in a stronger position to liaise with staff across the school and, if appropriate, with external specialists as well. Clearly it is easier for them to do this if they have direct responsibility for the pupils in question rather than having to work through their form tutors.

Some schools provide for pupils with special needs through a mixture of this arrangement and the previous one. They will have a core group who are the responsibility of the special centre and receive much of their teaching in it, plus other pupils who come to the centre for specific purposes on an individual or small group basis. This is generally found at secondary level where the numbers involved are greater. It is most usual in the case of physically handicapped pupils and those with moderate learning difficulties. Apart from helping to secure a good resource base for special needs provision, this combination offers considerable flexibility: different arrangements are possible for different pupils and – since pupils' needs change – for the same pupils at different times.

Special centre full-time

Pupils attend an ordinary school but receive all their teaching in a special class or unit. The school is often not their neighbourhood school: resources and expertise related to a particular set of learning difficulties are sometimes concentrated in a particular ordinary school which has then to service a wide catchment area. Thus, a special class for children with communication disorders may recruit from a dozen or more primary schools, whilst some secondary units, e.g., for physically handicapped pupils, have as their catchment area the entire district. This leads to all the problems of transport to and from school. It also means that children do not go to school with their neighbourhood peers and run a double risk of social isolation.

Special centres vary greatly, from special classes catering for half-a-dozen primary age children with speech and language difficulties to large secondary units catering for a hundred or more pupils with moderate learning difficulties. Some of the characteristics and organisational factors associated with special centres have been outlined above. What is distinctive is pupils' *full-time* presence in special centres: their entire curriculum is conceived within the framework of a special class or unit, and all their teaching takes place within its confines. This may be less of a departure from standard practice at primary level, where it is common for children to be taught by a single teacher, than it is at secondary level where such a concentration of teaching responsibility is unusual.

The major drawback of this arrangement is that it tends to minimise pupils' participation in the school. Physically they are part of the school and may have some social interactions at meal-times and in the playground, but that is all. School is essentially about teaching and learning, and exclusion from a school's mainstream class arrangements marks a significant isolation. Diminished participation in the life of the school can lead to marginal status, negative perceptions, and limited access to mainstream resources. Very careful planning is necessary if these outcomes are to be avoided, and the requisite planning is only likely to take place if the singular status of a full-time special centre is explicitly acknowledged.

Special school part-time, ordinary school part-time

Pupils placed in a special school and on its roll attend an ordinary school part-time. This can be for a couple of periods a week or it can be for the bulk of the school week. There is often a progression from an initial exploratory placement to spending a substantial period of time in the ordinary school, sometimes culminating in a full-time placement where the pupil is transferred to the roll of the ordinary school. Pupils may have individual timetables for these arrangements or they may divide their time between the two schools as part of a small group or even a whole class from a special school. Alternatively, pupils from an ordinary school may attend a special school for part of their time. This arrangement, which is less common, is usually for a specific purpose and for a limited period of time only.

Such arrangements are part of the general pattern of links between special schools and ordinary schools, which include staff and material resources as well as pupils. This is a recent development in special needs provision but is likely to grow. Depending on how it develops, it could be a major form of support for ordinary schools in teaching pupils with special needs. The topic is discussed in more detail in chapter 9.

Supporting The New School

Support from the local authority

Schools exist within a local authority structure. This defines the context in which they operate, and in which change takes place. The changes in view here entail major curriculum and organisational reform of schools, and they cannot take place without reference to the local authority. The interaction between the authority and school reform can be viewed from two perspectives. On the one hand, the local authority sets the limits of what is possible, through policy requirements and the allocation of resources: if it is policy, for instance, that pupils with visual impairment should be educated in a special school and resources are deployed accordingly, it is unlikely that a primary or secondary school will be able to establish provision for such pupils. On the other hand, the authority can provide support specifically to assist schools in their task of reform. This chapter is concerned with the latter perspective.

Schools require support services across a broad front if they are to make effective provision for pupils with special educational needs. This must include knowledge, advice, and the deployment of expertise that school staff do not have. It may encompass the provision of specific resources. This support can be provided directly to pupils or it can be given to teachers in the hope that pupils will benefit indirectly. It can take different organisational forms at local authority level and reach schools in a variety of ways.

Whatever it encompasses, and however it is organised and delivered, the importance of appropriate support to schools is undisputed. Quite apart from the absolute necessity for certain forms of support, staff morale is critically affected by the authority's stance on support. If official enthusiasm for building up special needs provision in ordinary schools is not matched by support in the form of the necessary resources, staff are less likely to give their full commitment than if policy is matched with a due allocation of resources. The Warnock Report regarded its proposals for the provision of advice and support as 'an indispensable condition for effective special educational provision in ordinary schools' (13.2).

The purpose of this chapter is to given an overview of the support services available to primary and secondary schools in the task of meeting special educational needs and to note some recent developments in them. These services come primarily, though not exclusively, from the local education authority. The key provision is the set of advisory and support services concerned with all aspects of teaching pupils with special needs. This includes as its major component staff responsible for pupils who have difficulty in learning, especially with reading; traditionally designated as the remedial service, they are now often restructured and designated as a learning support service. The set also includes peripatetic specialist staff concerned with pupils who have particular impairments. The Warnock Report recommended that these separate services should be combined, along with advisers, into a single unified service. In addition, account must be taken of educational psychologists, who have a key role in assessing pupils, and a range of other staff who provide essential support to ordinary schools.

LEARNING SUPPORT SERVICE

The most numerous group for which schools need support are the 18 per cent or so of pupils who are not the subject of a Statement but have a range of difficulties in learning. Schools have always had their 'slow learners' or 'remedial' pupils, and many have built up provision to meet their needs. Clunies-Ross and Wimhurst (1983), for instance, describe provision for slow learners in secondary schools in England and Wales at the beginning of the 1980s. As might be expected, they found wide variation in the organisation and content of provision and how it fitted into the school as a whole.

Schools' efforts for these pupils have been supported by local authority remedial services for many years. The first remedial centres were established at the end of the 1940s, but the principal growth in remedial services took place in the sixties when the concept of remedial education was taking root. By the end of the sixties, two-thirds of local authorities operated a remedial service (Laskier, 1985). These early services tended to concentrate on reading problems in primary schools. They were staffed by peripatetic remedial teachers who operated by withdrawing pupils from the classroom, often to a remedial centre quite separate from the school. There was little contact between remedial teacher and class teacher, particularly regarding pupils' learning. They supported schools by unburdening them of problems. In terms of Colby and Gulliver's (1985) ambulance service analogy, their function was to remove the casualties so that the teachers could get on with the battle.

The seventies were a time of upheaval and soul-searching for remedial staff. Initially, the expansion continued until most local authorities had a remedial service. At the same time, the notion of remedial education, which provided the rationale for the service, was under attack. It was based on a defect model of pupil failure and did not take account of the ways in which schools created learning difficulties, so that its prescriptions for individual treatment of pupils in isolation from the classroom were felt to be wide of the mark.

When the growing evidence that remedial provision made little difference to the pupils receiving it and the uncertainty over who exactly should be receiving it were added to this, there seemed to be little future for the remedial service as traditionally conceived. The Warnock Report proposed, in fact, that a meaningful distinction between remedial education and special education could not be sustained (3.39) and saw no place for the remedial service as presently constituted in its proposals for supporting ordinary schools (chapter 13). A further pressure on remedial services – if more were needed! – was the staffing cuts that followed from local authority economies in the late seventies.

The net result of all this has been a great deal of change. Remedial services have responded to the threat of redundancy by developing new roles and expanding their sphere of operation. Changes are still going on, not least because of the continuing efforts to implement the 1981 Act, and a static picture cannot yet be given. Two recent studies, however, highlight the principal changes and point the way forward. The first is based on a questionnaire to local authorities in 1983 (87 per cent response) followed by detailed case study of six authorities (Gipps, Gross and Goldstein, 1987). The second draws on a survey of authorities (74 per cent response) conducted by questionnaire and interview in 1984/85 (Moses, Hegarty and Jowett, 1988).

Virtually all local authorities operated a support service for pupils with learning difficulties and their teachers in ordinary schools. These went by a bewildering variety of titles: Gipps et al. list no fewer than 35. More than one-third of the titles used the word 'remedial'. Only one authority used the designation 'Special Education Advisory and Support Service' as recommended in the Warnock Report.

The variety of titles in use would suggest that authorities were restructuring their remedial service in many different ways. This is borne out in the management and staffing levels of the services. Responsibility for the service could be vested in an education officer, an adviser for special needs or a principal educational psychologist. The number of staff varied from five or even less to more than 50. The size of a service tended to reflect the size of the authority, but there were exceptions: some of the smallest authorities had large services whilst two of the largest had quite modest staffing levels. Moses et al. found that an important determinant of the size of a service was the type of work carried out. Services concerned predominantly with advising teachers tended to be smaller than those that spent most of their time teaching pupils.

It emerged clearly from both studies that staffing levels had improved considerably over the previous five years. The cuts made in the late seventies had generally been restored, and in some cases there had been a substantial increase in the number of staff. More than half of the authorities reported an overall increase. Furthermore, about a quarter planned staff increases in the near future. Where there was no overall change or a decrease in staffing level, this was often associated with substantial reorganisation in the direction of reducing the number of peripatetic teachers engaged in teaching pupils directly and an increase in the number of advisory teachers.

What of the actual work done by the services? How have they responded to the threat of impending redundancy? Moses et al. identified four main areas where changes have taken place: the clients of the service; area of work; mode of working; and age range covered.

1. *Clients*. The change here was from pupil to teacher. A majority of services still spent most of their time teaching pupils, but a good many were devoting themselves increasingly to teachers, advising and monitoring as opposed to teaching.

2. *Area of work*. The traditional focus on reading had widened to take in mathematics and other areas of the curriculum.

3. *Mode of working*. When staff from the service did teach, they were more likely to do so within the classroom. Withdrawal to a quiet area has been the long-established mode of working; a small number of services had abandoned this practice completely and most were doing less of it.

4. *Age range*. Secondary schools and their pupils were recipients of the service as well as primary.

Neither of the studies gives much information on the extent to which these changes are taking place, but both agree on their significance. It does seem likely that they signal the future shape of the service.

HEARING IMPAIRED SERVICE

Provision for pupils with hearing impairment is well established in ordinary schools. The first units were set up nearly 40 years ago, and many more have been established in the intervening period. These catered principally for pupils with partial hearing loss. Peripatetic services, initially concentrating on those with mild hearing loss, proliferated from the mid sixties onward.

Pupils with profound hearing loss remained in special schools for the most part, although early auditory training and advances in hearing-aid technology have weakened the distinction between partial hearing and profound deafness. This led some professionals in deaf education to question special schools for the deaf as the automatic placement for pupils with profound hearing loss. There was also some pressure from parents to provide opportunities for deaf children at school and pre-school level. The result was a modest growth in mainstream provision for pupils with profound hearing loss. This latter development clearly added to the responsibilities of local authorities in terms of support to ordinary schools since quite specialised skills and expert knowledge were called for.

Moses et al. (1988) found that all local authorities responding to a questionnaire in 1985 operated a support service for pupils with hearing impairment. Most were well established, with many in existence for 20 years or more. The services were made up of three components, not all of which were present in every case: peripatetic staff, units attached to ordinary schools, and a special school. The most common pattern was for the service to consist just of the peripatetic element, the units being an integral part of the schools to which they were attached. Some heads of service were responsible for unit provision as well, whilst in a few cases the service comprised all the authority's provision for hearing impairment, including a special school.

Staffing naturally reflected the type and structure of service. All were based on trained teachers of the deaf. Many engaged nursery nurses and other ancillary staff. Services generally had access to an appropriate range of specialists such as audiologists and audiometricians.

Staff working in these services spent about half of their time working in ordinary schools. The balance of the time was spent in special schools or in non-school activities such as working with pre-school children and their parents. The time in ordinary schools was spent monitoring pupils' hearing, diagnostic testing, supervising the use of aids, counselling, and giving careers guidance. Direct teaching was not common. Many of the activities in question cannot be carried out easily in the classroom, and it was common for pupils to be withdrawn for them. The support services tended to focus their efforts on pupils, but many advised teachers on teaching and classroom strategies and assisted them in monitoring pupils' progress.

VISUALLY IMPAIRED SERVICE

Local authority services for pupils with visual impairment have been relatively slow to develop. This is largely because of the lack of perceived need. (On the basis on an extensive national investigation Colbourne Brown and Tobin (1983) argue that not enough support is available and that there is a discrepancy between what professionals affirm to be available and what families say they receive.) Pupils with visual impairment have tended to be educated in special schools, often in the non-maintained sector, and impinged little on the local authority.

Despite encouragement from the Vernon Committee (DES, 1972), which urged authorities to experiment with integration, provision in ordinary schools grew very slowly. Peripatetic services grew slowly as well, aimed principally at pupils with lesser visual impairments (Jamieson et al., 1977). Special class provision remained at a low level up to the early 1980s. It should be acknowledged that the low incidence of visual handicap coupled with the scarcity of specialist teachers made it difficult in practical terms for local authorities to build up appropriate provision in ordinary schools.

Two factors in particular have conspired to change the situation and put pressure on authorities to build up provision. Firstly, the assessments conducted under the provisions of the 1981 Act require appropriate specialist advice to be taken. For pupils with visual impairment, this means having recourse to a qualified teacher for the blind. Where local authorities do not already employ such a person, they may find it more satisfactory to recruit one than to have to depend on non-authority staff. Such recruitment – or redeployment with training – may be only a small step, but it can be the nucleus of a larger team subsequently. Secondly, the general climate of opinion in favour of integration is leading toward more provision being made in ordinary schools. This in turn needs to be supported by appropriate services at local authority level.

The NFER survey referred to above (Moses et al., 1987) found that two-thirds of authorities had a specialist support service for the visually impaired in ordinary schools in 1985. (This was based on 77 authorities responding.) It was the smaller authorities, particularly the London boroughs, that were most likely not to have a service. Most services were very small, consisting of one or possibly two qualified teachers of the blind. In a few cases they belonged to a generic special needs service. This was perceived to be advantageous in reducing isolation and giving staff a professional context for their work.

Staff working in this service tended to spend less time in ordinary schools than their colleagues in other support services. This was because they spent more time working in special schools, and in other activities such as assessment, inservice training, and work with parents of young children. The time spent in ordinary schools was fairly evenly divided between pupils and teachers. Time with pupils tended *not* to be for teaching. Instead, the focus was on counselling, social skills, and the provision and management of aids. Time spent with teachers was devoted to explaining the nature of the pupil's visual impairment, helping the teacher to monitor progress, and advising on strategies for teaching, classroom management, and pupil mobility.

ADVISERS AND INSPECTORS

All local education authorities employ staff in an advisory capacity. As well as providing advice on a broad front, they are often responsible for monitoring the authority's educational provision and for developing new initiatives within it. Advisers and inspectors – there seems to be little difference in practice between the two designations – are principally associated with this work, and it is with them that this section is concerned.

The range of tasks carried out by advisory staff is exceedingly diverse. An early study by Bolam, Smith and Canter (1978) produced an awesome list: assisting in staff appointments; advising individual staff about professional and personal matters; evaluating probationers; advising in a single school or college on major organisational or curriculum changes; conducting general inspections; contributing to inservice training; planning and implementing authority-wide projects; advising on the design and furnishing of schools; and reporting to the authority. Hegarty and Pocklington (1981) found an equally broad range of tasks being carried out by special needs advisers. Even though their concern was confined to that aspect of advisers' work concerned with integration programmes, eight role components emerged: (i) staffing; (ii) advice to schools, on both curriculum and organisational matters; (iii) policy formulation; (iv) inservice training; (v) liaison, between school and the authority and between the education authority and other agencies; (vi) administrative duties; (vii) crisis intervention; and (viii) progress monitoring.

The above might appear to present an impossible array of tasks, with the corollary that only superhumans need apply for advisory work! Some advisers would no doubt agree with both statements, but a few caveats need to be entered. First, not all of these tasks are being done by every adviser. Some may spend most of their time giving curricular advice, whilst others almost never do so. When individual advisers are carrying out a range of tasks, the likelihood is that they will give higher priority and more time to some than to others. The same is true of the advisory service as a whole. Whatever dimension of advisory work is taken, services can be found which vary greatly in respect of it. Some services spend a considerable amount of time inspecting schools whilst others never do so, some give their highest priority to work in the classroom with teachers whilst others spend little time in classrooms, and so on. Finally, it should be remembered that advisory duties are undertaken by many other authority staff as well – education officers, advisory teachers, educational psychologists, and teacher centre leaders. This means that the tasks carried out by a given advisory service must be seen in the context of the functions assigned to other local authority colleagues.

Two NFER studies shed some light on the current situation of advisers. The first, which is still going on, is concerned with the advisory service as a whole. Interim findings point to four main role changes since services were restructured with local authority reorganisation in 1974:

1. The division between advisers and officers has become increasingly blurred, with the former especially taking on numerous administrative tasks.
2. Advisers spend less time working as subject specialists and more as generalists, concerned with the school as a whole and how it is managed.
3. Advisers spend a good deal of time implementing central curriculum initiatives.
4. The growth in the number of advisers and advisory teachers has meant greater management responsibility and less 'front line' work for senior staff.

One result of all this is that 'the job of advising is now so different from that of the competent classroom teacher that it can no longer be regarded as a simple extension of it' (Stillman and Grant, 1987). If true, this has major implications for recruitment and training (of advisers) as well as for their role perceptions.

The second study is the DES funded enquiry referred to earlier (Moses et al., 1987). It found a very substantial increase in the number of special needs advisers in post. In 1985, 90 per cent of responding authorities had at least one such adviser; in fact 30 per cent had two or more. Whilst advisory services generally were expanding, the rate of increase amongst special needs advisers has probably exceeded the average. This is due to the greater attention to special educational needs at authority level and to the administrative tasks highlighted by the 1981 Act.

The work carried out by five advisers was examined in detail. A common feeling was that their work was loosely defined and that they had a great deal of autonomy in deciding what they should do. This was welcomed for the flexibility it gave in responding to perceived needs, but it did leave staff vulnerable to setting idiosyncratic priorities and trespassing on colleagues' domains of work. Some central aspects of this work were common to all posts. They included: teacher support – reassuring teachers in their work of teaching pupils with special needs and generally sustaining morale; inservice training – running courses and contributing to them, assisting schools to develop their own training initiatives, and encouraging staff to take secondment; developing provision – particularly securing necessary resources; and administration – especially contributing to multiprofessional assessments and preparing Statements of special educational needs.

A UNIFIED SUPPORT SERVICE

There is no shortage of *type* of support service, even if the number of staff available to work in schools is sometimes limited. Support directly related to teaching can be provided by advisory teachers, specialist teachers in sensory impairment, and advisers. (Additionally, relevant advice can be given by educational psychologists, speech therapists, physiotherapists and careers officers – as discussed below.) Each of these groups has a distinctive contribution to make and must have a degree of professional autonomy in how they relate to schools and work within them.

There can be drawbacks in having numerous sources of advice. The support received by schools risks being fragmented, and teachers may be confused by conflicting emphases and approaches. From the providers' viewpoint, the separation between services means that there is little co-ordination between them, and it is unlikely that best use is made of scarce resources. For these reasons the Warnock Report recommended that unified services be established – 'every local education authority should restructure ... its existing advisory staff and resources to provide effective advice and support...through a unified service' (38.3). Few new staff were envisaged. The principal function of the new service was to co-ordinate existing efforts to help teachers. So it would be made up substantially of people already in post – advisers, advisory teachers, other specialist remedial teachers and practising teachers on part-time secondment. Educational psychologists were specifically excluded since the school psychological service was conceived as having a separate, albeit complementary, set of functions.

Progress toward unified services has been slow. Moses et al. (1988) found that one-fifth of authorities surveyed had combined existing support services to form a generic service. Some of these services encompassed a good deal of separate working still, but they did point the way forward. They facilitated co-ordination between the different specialist elements, and, in the more developed examples, provided support to schools on the basis of the identified educational needs of particular pupils rather than in accordance with handicap labels.

SCHOOL PSYCHOLOGICAL SERVICE

Psychologists have had a chequered career in the education service. The first appointment of a psychologist by an education authority was in 1913 – Cyril Burt at the London County Council. Numbers have grown since then, especially over the past 20 years, and most authorities now have a well-established school psychological service. (Some deliberately avoid the term 'school' in their designation to indicate that the service extends to clients outside the school sector.)

The status and functions of educational psychologists have been the subject of a great deal of debate and no little conflict. Their primary perceived role has been to assess pupils who have difficulty in learning with a view to determining what education they should receive, but for many years their formal status in this enterprise was marginal. The 1944 Act designated the medical officer as the person who would decide for the local authority whether a child needed special educational treatment. As educational psychologists grew in number and established a power base in local authorities, they gradually took over this task until they came to be widely perceived as the 'gatekeepers' to special education. The 1981 Act gave them a formal legislative role in the assessment process. (In Scotland educational psychologists had enjoyed legislative status since the 1960s.)

The Warnock Report estimated the ratio of psychologists to the school population as 1 to 11,000 in England and Wales and 1 to 4,000 in Scotland. This contrasted with the Summerfield recommendation of 1 per 10,000 (DES, 1968) and its own of 1 per 5,000. The number of educational psychologists in post has increased dramatically since that time. Whilst national figures are not available, Moses et al. (1988) found that the great majority of authorities were employing more educational psychologists in 1984/85 than in 1978. The average increase in those authorities employing more staff was almost one-third of the existing establishment.

Several studies have described the work done by educational psychologists – Wright and Payne (1979), Wedell and Lambourne (1980), and Hegarty and Pocklington (1981). Two things stand out from these accounts: the wide range of tasks carried out by psychologists; and the focus, none the less, on assessing and treating individual children. The three studies identified seven, eight, and ten components of psychologists' work respectively! These ranged over assessment, training, advising teachers, working with families, and carrying out research.

The predominant activity in terms of amount of time and priority given to it was assessing children and contributing to placement decisions. Some psychologists have reacted against this role. When coupled with heavy caseloads of children for referral, it meant a relatively static involvement in children's difficulties. The pattern often was to see a child just once, probably outside the classroom setting, administer some tests, make a recommendation and then not see the child again. To add to their discomfiture, psychologists were then criticised by teachers for making educational prescriptions they did not have to implement and that sometimes bore little relation to classroom realities.

How have psychologists fared since the 1981 Act? Does the expansion in numbers enable them to play a more active part in suporting ordinary schools? It is still too early to be definite but the indications are that much of the additional staff time is taken up with implementing the Act. Ironically, this is in spite of the fact that the role of the psychologist in assessment and placement decisions has diminished in some respects.

Under the previous arrangements psychologists had a key *de facto* role and effectively controlled the procedures by which children were ascertained for special educational treatment, whereas now their input is only one amongst several and is not accorded any special priority. The formality of the Act however, and the detailed procedures associated with it, have generated a great deal of extra work for psychologists. When a child is formally assessed under the Act, psychological evidence must be obtained in written form from an educational psychologist. In the event that special educational provision is deemed necessary – on the basis of all the evidence obtained – the written submissions become part of the Statement that is maintained on the child.

Whilst the number of children going through these formal procedures and receiving a Statement is not appreciably greater than the number being dealt with under the old arrangements, the amount of time involved is considerably greater. In some authorities psychologists are also charged with collating the evidence from the different sources.

Whilst the formal assessment role predominates, some psychological services and many individual psychologists have been developing closer links with ordinary schools. This often entails working at a whole school level, where the psychologist can make a number of key contributions:

- question pupil-centred models of learning difficulty and help teachers to identify ways in which their school is making it difficult for pupils to learn
- advise on teaching strategies and resources and contribute to curriculum development in a general way
- give detailed technical assistance in drawing up programmes based on task analysis and behavioural objectives
- monitor, or assist in devising methods for monitoring, provision related to pupils with special needs
- contribute to inservice training in the above or in other areas such as working with parents.

Psychologists can also work in a more focussed way with individual pupils and their teachers, e.g., working out with the teacher the classroom significance of formal assessment findings or helping the teacher to monitor a pupil's learning or behaviour systematically over a period of time.

However desirable this kind of support from the psychological service might be, it is still relatively uncommon. Many schools rarely see a psychologist, and many psychologists do not have the time to build up the kind of informed partnership with schools that it requires. Apart from psychologists' assessment caseloads, there are other factors that inhibit the development of this role. Many psychologists have little teaching experience and may not have the competence or the credibility to make significant inputs to curriculum practice in a school.

A more substantial difficulty is the potential overlap with the advisory and support service. In principle, the psychological service has a distinctive sphere of operation in the giving of advice to schools on the psychological aspects of education and individual development. In practice, this tends to overlap with advisory, training, and even administrative functions carried out by colleagues. This can lead to an ambiguity in the lines of support to schools, which is largely unresolved at the moment. Schools may benefit from having access to a range of sources of advice and support, but there is a danger of creating confusion over who is responsible for what. It might be felt too that even partial duplication of support services in this way is not the most effective way of using limited resources.

OTHER STAFF

Ordinary schools should not be looking over their shoulders at special schools in building up provision for special needs, but they have to be aware that certain specialist staff are readily available to special schools. If their provision is not to be found wanting, they must find ways of ensuring that corresponding expertise is available as appropriate in the ordinary school setting. This section looks briefly at speech therapists, physiotherapists, and careers officers in this context. It also refers to the deployment of ancillary staff, since this often determines whether plans for pupils with special needs are turned into effective provision on the ground.

Speech therapists

The provision of speech therapy to ordinary schools is beset with problems: speech therapists are employed by health authorities, not education authorities; there are too few of them; and their training does not equip them fully for work in educational settings. These difficulties notwithstanding, speech therapists have an important contribution to make to provision for pupils with special educational needs in ordinary schools.

Their expertise is in language and communication – many regard their title as a misnomer since it places too much emphasis on speech, which is only one of their concerns. When children exhibit a difficulty in language, they can contribute to initial assessment, draw up individual programmes of work and carry out specific therapies or other work. They can also be a general resource to schools on all matters to do with language difficulty. Hegarty and Pocklington (1982) give detailed descriptions of speech therapists at work in ordinary schools (see also Webster and McConnell, 1987).

Most ordinary schools have little access to speech therapists, unless they have a language unit catering for pupils with significant language difficulties. In the latter case, speech therapists are assigned to the school on a regular, sessional basis and may be able to provide a service to the school as a whole. Many pupils who would benefit from speech therapy do not receive it. A recent report estimated the likely incidence and prevalence of persons in the United Kingdom with speech and language disorders, and concluded that the figures on which current service planning is based seriously underestimate the true situation (Enderby and Philipp, 1986).

Physiotherapists

Physiotherapists are concerned with assessing physical skills and mobility and making appropriate remedial interventions. Like speech therapists, they are employed by health authorities and are also in short supply. Most work within the health service, usually in hospital settings. Those that work in the school sector are concerned primarily with pupils with physical handicap and generally work in special schools. Their work consists of assessing pupils, providing treatment, informing teachers of pupils' capacities and liaising between them and medical colleagues.

Providing physiotherapy in ordinary schools calls for major changes in how physiotherapists work. They probably have to do without specialist equipment and work in a physically unsuitable environment. Physiotherapy has to fit in around the academic timetable, and in secondary schools may be confined to lunchtimes. Physiotherapists may well have to delegate much of their work to unqualified ancillary staff. These changes in working practice are alien to the professional ethos of many physiotherapists, but there are examples of successful practice where effective provision has been made despite these constraints. Davies (1980) describes one such in North Wales where there was an extensive programme of educating pupils with physical handicap in their own neighbourhood schools.

Careers officers

Careers officers give information to young people on career entry requirements and job opportunities and help them to make appropriate choices. Young people with special needs are likely to benefit from specialist advice because of the diversity of training opportunities after the age of 16 and the possibility that there will be greater difficulty in matching them to available jobs. There are specialist careers officers who have a detailed knowledge of the relevant opportunities and are experienced in advising young people with special needs. They are relatively scarce, however, and certainly too few to cater for the full range of special needs (Parker, 1984).

How is the careers service to respond to this situation and ensure that the enhanced educational provision that young people with special needs receive in schools is matched by a corresponding increment in careers advice? Rather than seeking to build up the number of specialist careers officers, an alternative strategy would be to extend the knowledge and skills of careers officers generally. There would still be need of specialists but their contribution would sit within the context of a more comprehensive basic service. This could go hand in hand with the careers service devoting more time to advising careers teachers within schools and helping staff to make their leavers' programmes more relevant to young people with special needs.

Ancillary staff

Ancillary staff are included here because, whilst not a service in the same way as the other groups, and often part of the schools' establishment, their availability to schools is usually determined directly by the local authority. Some authorities have set formulae for allocating ancillaries – so many hours' ancillary time per pupil with specific needs. Others operate in a more *ad hoc* way, responding to pressure or representations made.

However they are allocated, ancillary staff are one of the most important – and often least regarded – forms of support to ordinary schools in meeting special educational needs. They can carry out a wide range of functions: providing physical care; acting as para-professional to implement programmes drawn up by speech therapists and physiotherapists; and contributing to pupils' education, both indirectly – by preparing teaching materials, marking work set, helping with practical work – and directly by engaging in teaching activities under a teacher's instruction. Quite apart from the intrinsic value of these functions, when ancillaries carry them out teachers are freed from doing them and have more time for teaching.

How the special school can help

INTRODUCTION

There are close on 2,000 special schools in Britain, providing education for 135,000 pupils. They employ nearly 20,000 teachers as well as numerous other staff. This constitutes a sizeable pool of experience in dealing with pupils who have special educational needs. In addition, there has been considerable investment in the plant of special schools. Some older buildings may be substandard but many special schools had been built and fitted out to a high standard; some have lifts, swimming pools, and other specialist areas and equipment as appropriate.

Special schools are clearly a major resource in the education of pupils with special needs. They are, moreover, going to be part of the pattern of provision for some time to come. Even if it were not evident that progress toward the necessary reform of the ordinary school is slow, there are two further considerations that would confirm this. Firstly, the special school sector constitutes a complex *system* of educational provision, and it is not possible to dismantle it overnight and re-establish equivalent provision in ordinary schools. System change, even if imposed, needs time and experience in order to consolidate. New structures have to be built up gradually and modified in the light of experience; attitude change cannot be pushed beyond a certain level if it is to lead to real change; working relationships and practices must be given space to develop.

Secondly, there is no intention in practice to impose change or to shut down large numbers of special schools in the short term. Whilst the new legislation has a presumption in favour of integration and should lead to improved provision in ordinary schools for pupils with special needs, it does not call for a specific programme of special school closures. Neither is there a great groundswell in favour of shutting down special schools. Whilst some people feel that progress in switching resources from special to ordinary has been far too slow, it is commonly held that changes should be made gradually.

For these various reasons we can expect to see special schools about for a good many years to come, though they may be different in some respects from schools of today. It is not actually necessary to take sides in the argument about whether there should still be special schools or not, in order to adopt a positive stance and capitalise on what they have to offer. At the moment special schools have precisely what ordinary schools lack – experience in dealing with pupils who have special educational needs. The best special schools have a strength in adapting and developing the curriculum, in teaching techniques such as task analysis and direct instruction, in working with parents and in linking with local employers and post-school training agencies. Ordinary schools can only gain from tapping into this expertise.

The purpose of the chapter, in keeping with this pragmatic stance, is to outline the range of ways in which special schools and ordinary schools can work together fruitfully. It draws on recent work at NFER. As part of a larger study of support for ordinary schools in the task of meeting special needs, a survey of special schools in England and Wales was conducted to find out what links they had with ordinary schools. A high proportion of special schools had, in fact, established working links with one or more ordinary schools. These involved pupils and staff, in both directions. Some special schools acted as resource centres, providing information and consultancy to neighbouring schools and contributing to inservice training activities. This account is prefaced with a discussion of the reasons for the emergence of this novel form of educational organisation – schools are after all jealous of their identity and their autonomy – and concludes with a look at some of the implications for future practice.

WHY LINKS?

Cynics will say that special schools' enthusiasm for links with ordinary schools owes more to survival instincts than to anything else! As numbers decline, they must find new roles and functions if they are to avoid being closed. Doubtless there is some truth in this, but it is not the whole story by any means; nor is it particularly fair to the many schools and local authority officers who are trying to make better use of the available resources. Link schemes have in fact developed for a variety of reasons, some at authority level and some at the level of the individual school or head teacher.

Authority level

Two types of consideration come into play where local authorities are concerned: one where links are a response to falling school rolls; and one where links are positively sought in their own right and planned as an integral feature of an authority's entire special needs provision.

Falling rolls – in both special schools and ordinary schools – have proved to be a mixed blessing for local education authorities. They provide opportunities to rationalise provision and deploy resources to better effect. Frequently, however, these advantages can only be gained by means of school closures which are politically unpopular and create a host of new problems. If closures do not take place, small schools may contract to the point of non-viability as they lose staff with particular expertise or teacher–pupil ratios become disproportionately expensive. Special schools are particularly vulnerable in this respect since teachers with specialist curriculum skills are in short supply anyway.

Some local authorities have responded to this situation by encouraging the establishment of link schemes. Instead of eliminating posts – and risking possible school closures – they have maintained staffing levels at special schools by giving teachers a range of additional functions such as those involved in running a link scheme or a resource centre. Since rolls are also falling in ordinary schools, they too may have staff who need to be redeployed. Again, one of the ways of achieving this is to involve staff in a link scheme with a special school. It is worth noting that ordinary schools are more willing, as well as possibly more able, to forge links and receive pupils from special schools when their numbers are falling. When schools were still expanding and many experienced pressure on accommodation, it would have been much more difficult to organise such schemes.

Aside from falling rolls, there are many instances where local authorities make a positive choice for link arrangements and introduce them as an integral part of their special needs provision. The first is when an authority has identified the need for a resource centre in special education and decides that the most appropriate way of establishing such a centre is to build it on the base of a special school. The functions of such centres, which include collecting information and providing advice, can be a valid extension of what some special schools are already doing.

The second instance concerns the Education Act 1981, which has led some authorities to develop link schemes. Ordinary schools have an obligation under the Act to assess their pupils' special needs, make appropriate provision for them and secure the extra resources required for pupils who are the subject of a Statement. Whilst authorities have support services to assist schools and teachers in these tasks, virtually all are very hard pressed and would benefit from more assistance. Under these circumstances, some have turned to special schools as an additional resource and see link arrangements as one means whereby ordinary schools can be helped to discharge their duties under the Act.

Finally, some authorities have adopted formal policy documents outlining their special needs provision. Typically, these lay down guiding principles, detail different forms of provision available within the authority, specify assessment and placement procedures, and note significant developments for the future. Such policy documents can incorporate link schemes and ensure that they have a coherent and planned place within the range of provision for special needs in the authority.

Probably the best known example of such a policy document is that produced by the Inner London Education Authority (ILEA, 1985). Entitled *Educational Opportunities for All?*, it is the report of a committee set up to review the authority's provision for meeting special educational needs and to make recommendations for improving it. Amongst the numerous recommendations was one that each day special school should be formally linked with an appropriate primary or secondary school (3.18.12). This would:

1. Facilitate interaction between both teachers and pupils across the two sectors.
2. Provide assistance to ordinary schools in meeting special educational needs.
3. Enrich the curriculum and resources of the special schools.

In addition, special schools should, where possible, link in with the proposed new 'clusters' of educational provision in an area. A cluster comprises the primary and secondary schools in a locality along with their associated under-five provision and links with tertiary provision. Amongst other benefits, this form of organisation is designed to enable schools 'to work together to develop mutually supportive arrangements to meet special educational needs and provide a focus for the deployment of supporting services' (3.16.22). If special schools join the clusters, this allows the possibility of even greater coherence in the planning and delivery of services. In particular, it would 'encourage a move towards joint working arrangements with other facilities, be a necessary stage in developing as local resource centres and an important first step in developing the process of integration' (3.18.13). The report also makes a number of specific recommendations for schools that provide for children with physical and sensory disabilities. Regardless of whether they are day or boarding schools, they should be linked with unit and peripatetic teaching provision and should support more pupils in ordinary schools. They should become part of a unified service catering flexibly for all pupils wherever they are receiving their education.

School level

Many link schemes are, of course, the brainchild of individual head teachers or other staff members and only exist because of particular local initiatives. As with the case of authority-originated schemes motives can be mixed, but essentially the same pattern – of either responding to events or attempting to shape them – emerges. Falling rolls and all the threats to survival that they represent are certainly a potent factor in many cases, but there are other quite separate considerations too that are rooted in concern for children's educational benefit.

Apart from their intrinsic significance, these more positive considerations are important for giving the lie to those sociologists who view special education in a simplistic, one-dimensional way. Special education has often been seen as a form of social benevolence, and still is in many respects. (Cf. fundraising campaigns, especially prevalent in the fields of blindness, and physical and mental handicap, which rely on heart-tugging images of helplessness.) Those commentators who take issue with this view of special education are perfectly right so to do: it is misguided in principle, and factually incorrect. It is misguided because all children have the right to education and no child should have to depend on charity for access to education. It is incorrect because special education is a social product and as such has been shaped by a complex mix of moral, cultural, economic, and political factors; social benevolence has been only one strand amongst many in shaping the pattern of special education.

The reaction to the benevolence view often goes to the other extreme, picturing special education as a conspiracy against a dispossessed and helpless group and at best an arrangement that serves the vested interests of the professionals involved. It would be naive to ignore professionals' self-interest but, in fact, significant advances have come about precisely through disinterested concern on the part of professionals. This is well illustrated by the emergence of link schemes: many stem from an explicit concern for children's benefit, and some indeed are detrimental to the career interests of the very staff who inaugurate them.

Some of the early link schemes were undoubtedly established by head teachers of special schools who felt that their school was under threat. With the growing body of opinion in favour of integration, many special schools did not feel confident about the future, and some saw a possible salvation in the development of link schemes.

By expanding their work and taking on a range of new functions they would become less dependent on gross pupil numbers. This could be viewed as straightforward diversification in response to market forces – if your main area of work is under threat of decline, you seek out other areas in order to stay in business. In the event, these fears have been groundless, or at least premature, since the expected contraction of the special school system has not material-ised. Special school numbers as a proportion of the schoolgoing population have stayed relatively constant over the past 15 years, and the rate of special school closures has been in line with the drop in the total school roll. To some extent, however, what matters here is what people believe, and there can be no doubt but that the possibility of contraction and even demise has concentrated minds in a very salutary way!

As opposed to all of this, there are many link schemes rooted in an unambiguous concern for children's educational benefit. Jowett, Hegarty and Moses (1988) document instances where special schools have taken the initiative in setting up schemes where pupils spend increasing periods of time away from the special school. Such schemes reduce the amount of teaching done in special schools; they reduce the time pupils spend in special schools; and they are likely to reduce the number of pupils on special school rolls. The aim is to maximise the amount of time that pupils spend in the mainstream, with the link perceived as a progressive series of steps leading ultimately to a full-time, permanent placement in an ordinary school. The concern throughout such schemes is to desegregate pupils as much as possible but to do so in a gradual, supportive way while ensuring that their educational needs continue to be met.

These links are dynamic in character, and as a result have led to some startling developments. In the first instance it may be just one or a small number of pupils that is judged likely to benefit from spending time in an ordinary school and in due course transferring to its roll. As time goes by, the number grows, sometimes to a point where there are so few pupils remaining in the special school that its viability is called into question. Jowett et al. report several cases where this has led to a special school being absorbed within an ordinary school and ceasing to have an independent existence. In each case observed, the stimulus for these developments came from within the special school. Motivated by a conviction that their pupils would be better catered for in an ordinary school rather than by professional self-interest, special school staff entered into link schemes with the closure of their own school as the likely end in view. They saw the link arrangements as a period of transition designed to ensure that the ordinary school and its teachers were adequately prepared and to establish the requisite support for pupils with special needs in the ordinary school.

Another context for establishing link schemes has to do with capitalising on the reservoir of expertise in special schools. The Warnock Report recommended that some special schools in every education authority should become 'centres of specialist expertise' and act as a resource for other schools in the teaching of pupils with special needs. This idea has been in currency for some time and was at once attractive and challenging to special schools. The attraction was that it gave them the chance to display their wares and show mainstream colleagues the expertise they possessed. It also enabled them to make their expertise available to many more pupils. The challenge was to develop new ways of working, possibly in situations over which they had little control, to have the confidence to display their skills in public, and inevitably to run the risk of failure. Not every school is motivated by these considerations – and some are properly modest about the expertise they possess! – but enough are fired by the challenges for local authorities to be able to include special school outreach as one of the ways in which they support ordinary schools in the task of meeting special educational needs.

A final point worth noting is that, at the present time, ordinary schools and special schools complement each other neatly in terms both of need and of opportunity. Ordinary schools need more expertise in teaching pupils with special educational needs, whether it be because they are now educating pupils who might have previously gone to a special school or because they are more aware of the failure to learn of many pupils already at the school. Special schools possess the necessary expertise, and have moreover – because of falling rolls – a need to deploy it in fresh fields. This conjuncture of interests is fortuitous, and furnishes a powerful motivation for all concerned to develop linking arrangements.

TYPES OF LINK

Link arrangements are as diverse as the schools they bring into partnership. There are some recognisable patterns however. With the exception of two extreme situations, most link arrangements can be characterised in terms of the *subject* of the arrangement, i.e., that which forms the bridge between the two schools. If we accept the crude model of schools represented in the diagram we can see that the subjects of link arrangements will be pupils, staff, and resources, either singly or in combination. The exceptional situations, which can perhaps be located at opposite ends of a notional

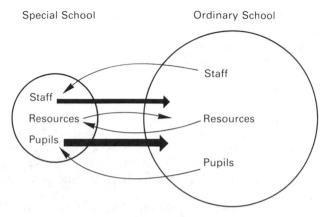

Special School   Ordinary School

Staff

Staff

Resources   Resources

Pupils

Pupils

Figure 9.1 Links between schools

continuum, occur when the special school acts purely as a resource centre, possibly serving a large number of schools, and when the special school is absorbed into an ordinary school and becomes an integral part of it.

Pupils

As is evident from figure 9.1 (where the thickness of the lines indicates the relative frequency of occurrence), pupil movement from special school to ordinary school is the most common form of link arrangement. This takes place in various ways: pupils may go out individually, in small groups or even as a whole class; they may attend the ordinary school for a few periods only or for the bulk of the school week; the link may be for a specific, limited purpose only or it may be exploratory with a view to extending the time spent in the ordinary school. In a few cases the movement of pupils is in the opposite direction with pupils going from an ordinary school to a special school. This is usually for a limited time and for a specific purpose. It tends to arise when special school teachers draw attention to individual pupils in the ordinary school and propose a short-term intervention for them that is best provided in the special school.

What does all this pupil movement signify for the ordinary school? It is clear that it impinges on them and contributes toward their life in different ways. The most obvious consideration, perhaps, is that the ordinary school is encountering pupils with a wider range of special needs than it has been accustomed to and must take steps to accommodate them, both physically and academically. Where pupils have impaired mobility, for instance, some modification to the school buildings may be necessary, or it may be advisable to alter the pattern of pupil movement around the school. Apart from the small number of cases where an entire special school class arrives and is taught *en bloc*, pupils coming from the special school have to be fitted into the academic structure of the ordinary school. This may be based on mixed ability groups or on some form of ability/achievement-related groupings. There may or may not be support from the special school. Regardless of how it is carried out or resourced, if an ordinary school takes on pupils from a special school it is thereby accepting a responsibility for their education and must ensure that appropriate teaching is available for them.

Considerable demands are placed on the ordinary school by the arrival of pupils from a special school. The balance of advantage is not all one way however. Ordinary schools stand to gain a great deal from the presence of these pupils. The very task of gearing themselves up to teach these pupils appropriately serves to heighten awareness of the special needs of pupils already in the school, and to suggest ways in which their education could be enhanced. Many ordinary schools have large numbers of pupils who are not well taught and who fail to reach their educational potential. These are often major beneficiaries of link arrangements as teachers in ordinary schools become more aware of their particular learning needs and more skilled in catering for them.

Staff

The second component of a link arrangement is staff, both teachers and classroom assistants. Again the main pattern of movement is from the special school to the ordinary school. Special school teachers can engage in three broad sets of activities when they go to an ordinary school: (i) teaching; (ii) supporting mainstream colleagues; and (iii) monitoring the link arrangements.

The teaching may be geared to their 'own' pupils or may extend to pupils from the ordinary school. As noted above, in a few cases teachers take a whole class group from the special school and teach them in the ordinary school. This is simply a change of location to begin with but it can be used to familiarise pupils with the daunting surroundings of a large ordinary school and pave the way for placing them in mainstream classes. When pupils from a special school are placed in mainstream classes, the special school teachers may still be involved in teaching them, though this is often indirect or on a shared basis. Thus, a teacher from a special school may join mainstream colleagues in team teaching and take particular responsibility within the team for special needs. The total group of pupils being taught in this way may include several from the special school. The special school teacher will have some concern for these but, in keeping with the philosophy and practice of team teaching, will not confine attention to them and will indeed function as an ordinary teacher in respect of many other pupils. Sometimes pupils from the special school join an existing class of lower-attaining pupils; in these cases the special school teacher may take on at least a partial responsibility for this mainstream class.

Much of the above entails a measure of support for mainstream colleagues, particularly when special school teachers take responsibility for special needs in team teaching. They can also supply a great deal of direct help that is not concerned with pupils from the special school but is oriented, rather, to any pupil in the school who has difficulty in learning. They can act as a general source of information on teaching such pupils; they will be familiar with the relevant literature and curriculum materials and may well know something of local services for children and families in difficulty. They can advise on particular pupils who are presenting difficulty. These may be pupils on the main school roll whom they identify themselves or ones that mainstream staff bring to notice. The advice can range from general guidelines on handling unruly classes to specific suggestions for managing particular pupils' learning or even drawing up a programme of work for pupils who are not responding to normal class teaching. They can also provide an important level of inservice training for their mainstream colleagues, either formally through lectures and workshops or informally when they discuss individual pupils and situations or engage in other professional interaction.

Finally, special school teachers involve themselves in monitoring the progress of the link arrangements. There will be need of extensive liaison when the programme is being set up. This may have to continue for some time as working practices that are quite novel for both parties are established. A degree of liaison and supervision will still be necessary when the programme is running. A close eye must be kept on the progress of individual pupils and adjustments made as necessary. Special school staff must be careful not to take over the responsibility of mainstream colleagues in this regard but equally they must often retain a measure of responsibility for certain pupils.

Classroom assistants may also spend time working out of the special school. This is usually to support particular pupils from the special school who are spending part of their time in ordinary school classes. They tend to carry out their usual range of activities, though possibly on a more restricted basis than if they were working in a special school – physical care, assistance with classroom work, and general support.

The final aspect of staff movement is when teachers go from an ordinary school to a special school. This is relatively uncommon but can be extremely useful none the less. A major problem found by many special schools is how to provide an adequate range of curriculum. Their staffing establishments may be too low or they may be unable to attract enough subject specialist teachers. Whatever the reasons, the results are the same: some pupils in special schools have their learning difficulties compounded by being taught by teachers who have a limited grasp of the subject area. Subject specialists from the ordinary school are well placed to help; if they adapt their teaching appropriately they can ensure that special school classes receive proper teaching in areas such as science and music. Special schools are the main beneficiaries here but there is likely to be considerable spin-off benefit for ordinary schools. Once again, the experience of teaching pupils who have considerable difficulties in learning can be the occasion of significant professional development for many staff which then feeds into their teaching in the ordinary school. They become more sensitive to the learning difficulties of lower-attaining pupils in the ordinary school and are likely to find that teaching approaches developed for classes in the special school have ready application in the ordinary school as well.

Resources

In addition to pupils and staff, link arrangements can also involve the transfer, or sharing, of material resources. This is often a major benefit to special schools, as when they make use of laboratories and craft workshops in an ordinary school. When pupils from a special school spend time in an ordinary school they often take with them curriculum materials and handicap-specific items of equipment. There can be significant benefits for the ordinary school as well. Some special schools have superior facilities, such as swimming pools and PE areas, that can be used by linking ordinary schools. Occasionally they have items of microcomputer equipment that are far more sophisticated than anything possessed by the ordinary school; these again can be used to the advantage of the latter's pupils. The most significant benefit, however, is likely to be in the curriculum. Special schools have a wide range of curriculum material geared to teaching pupils with special needs. Much of this will be useful in ordinary schools too, and teachers there who are faced with pupils who have difficulties in learning can draw on it to focus and enrich their teaching.

So far we have been considering link arrangements in terms of how they involve pupils, teachers, or resources separately from each other. This is artificial to an extent and has been done in order to simplify description. In reality, link arrangements are not so easily categorised. A particular link may involve elements of each but in quite a different combination to another link. If a special school and an ordinary school are sharing the education of any sizeable number of pupils they will almost certainly be sharing staff as well. When curriculum materials are shared between schools they are usually introduced to the second school by teachers from the first.

There are two further situations that, though not links in the same way as the other arrangements described here, are relevant in the context of providing support for ordinary schools in teaching pupils with special educational needs. These are the two exceptions referred to earlier – the special school as resource centre and the special school as absorbed into an ordinary school. If we place the various types of link arrangement along a continuum in terms of closeness or degree of union between the two partners, these would represent the two extremes: the resource centre function does not entail any particular union, whereas absorption means total union. By analogy with the business world, they could perhaps be regarded as consultancy and merger respectively.

Resource centre

Special schools that act as resource centres capitalise on their concentration of expertise and resources to provide a service to neighbouring schools. Such a service is usually to a number of schools rather than just one. It consists of giving information and advice to ordinary schools on matters related to teaching pupils with special educational needs. It does not preclude other, closer links but can take place without them. A special school does not have to have staff or pupil links in order to provide advice or disseminate information to other schools.

In some respects, special schools that act as a resource in this way are taking on aspects of the work of various other agencies – advisers, peripatetic support services, teachers' centres. They have the advantage in doing so of being able to base themselves on actual, current experience of teaching pupils with pronounced special needs. A potential drawback is that many of the pupils for whom ordinary schools need advice have less serious problems, and advice may be misdirected as a consequence. Special schools sometimes lack the necessary staffing flexibility as well. Teachers cannot be effective consultants if they are teaching for the entire week. A sufficient amount of non-contact time must be built into their timetables.

From the perspective of ordinary school staff, the resource centre function can be extremely valuable. They receive help from fellow teachers and, unlike the case of some of the formally designated support agencies, enjoy quick and informal access to them. The help they receive is also likely to have a strong classroom focus. On the debit side, there is the danger, present with all forms of external support, that the special school is merely enabling the ordinary school to shelve responsibility for pupils with special needs and delay building up appropriate curriculum provision for all its pupils. This is, of course, very much a question of how the support is provided. If the approach of the special school is one of tackling individual problems and looking for 'cures', ordinary school staff may defer to the expertise of the specialist. The special school can carry out the resource function in a different way however. If the orientation is one of prevention rather than cure, of helping mainstream staff to solve problems themselves instead of solving problems for them, they are more likely to assist the ordinary school to build up its own provision.

Absorption

The situation when a special school is absorbed into an ordinary school is at quite the other extreme from this advisory and resource centre role. As noted above, it is relatively rare – as yet – but is no less significant for that. Essentially, it means that the special school no longer exists as an independent entity. Needless to say, this can be traumatic for special school staff, but the implications for the ordinary school are rather more worthy of note since they are both long term and uncertain.

Two scenarios are possible when a special school is absorbed by an ordinary school: the special school retains a quasi-independent existence within the ordinary school; or it discards any separate identity and becomes an integral part of the ordinary school. The first scenario has little to commend it. The special school becomes, in effect, a department of the ordinary school with rather an odd status. This probably manages to combine the worst of both worlds since the erstwhile special school suffers the disadvantage of losing autonomous status without gaining the advantages of being in the mainstream. It is to be hoped that when this occurs it is only a temporary stage. The long-term goal must be the second scenario, where the expertise and the resources of the special school become an integral part of the educational provision of the ordinary school. It is not a matter of fitting an extra attachment to the ordinary school but of redesigning and restructuring it so that it functions in a different way. This restructured school will, in particular, be able to respond flexibly and from a base of expertise to a far wider range of educational needs.

LINK ARRANGEMENTS IN PRACTICE

So much for the diversity of *possible* links. Here we look at what is happening in practice. The NFER study referred to above is the key source of information here. All special schools in 26 local authorities in England and Wales were surveyed in 1985 to find out if they were involved in link arrangements and, if so, what form they took. A response of 90 per cent, representing 268 schools, was obtained.

Table 9.1 *Special schools involved in links*

	No	%
Current link	197	74
Plans for a link	26	10
Previous link	5	2
No involvement in links	40	15
	268	

The most striking fact to emerge from the survey was the scale on which links were taking place. As table 9.1 shows, three-quarters of the special schools were currently involved in a link of some kind whilst a further one-tenth were planning to set up links in the future. There is no reason to suppose that the special schools in the authorities selected for the survey were atypical. It would appear, then, that a considerable majority of special schools in England and Wales are engaged in a link of some kind with an ordinary school and, moreover, that the number engaged in this way is still growing.

Where links were established they were typically multi-faceted. Of the 197 schools reporting a current link, over two-thirds involved both pupils and teachers. Table 9.2 shows also that one quarter of the links involved pupils only whereas very few were restricted to teachers only.

Most pupil movement was from a special school to an ordinary school though there was some in the reverse direction as well. A total of 167 special schools were sending pupils out to an ordinary

120 *Meeting Special Needs in Ordinary Schools*

Table 9.2 *Pupil–teacher involvement in links*

	No	%
Both pupils and teachers involved	136	69
Pupils only	52	26
Teachers only	9	5
	197	

school whereas 116 were receiving pupils from an ordinary school. The gross figures do not give a realistic comparison, however, because the scale of the two operations was rather different.

Movement out of the special school was by far the most substantial, involving some 1,600 pupils. On a national basis this would suggest that about six per cent of pupils attending a special school are spending some time in an ordinary school. (This is an estimate only since the school rolls are not given.) Nearly twice as many pupils went out as members of a group than went as individuals. Most pupils spent relatively short periods of time in the ordinary school, though they were likely to spend longer if they went out on an individual basis. A small minority were in fact spending substantial periods of the week in an ordinary school.

Movement in the other direction, *to* a special school, was more restricted in scale, though the number of special schools receiving pupils in this way should be noted. At 116 it constitutes almost half the total number of special schools sampled. The number of pupils involved in this 'reverse' movement was typically small, as was the amount of time spent in the special school by a given pupil from the ordinary school.

The movement of staff between schools seems to have been more evenly divided. About one-third of special schools had staff going out to ordinary schools on a weekly basis. (This involved 200 teachers and 83 classroom assistants from 95 schools.) The nature and duration of these visits varied greatly. A quarter of the teachers spent at least one full day a week out in an ordinary school. The main activities undertaken, in order of frequency, were:

- teaching mixed classes of mainstream and special school pupils
- advising mainstream colleagues
- working with pupils from the special school.

Teaching mainstream classes (not containing special school pupils) and liaising with mainstream staff accounted for relatively little time.

Rather more than one-third of the special schools sampled were receiving visits from ordinary school staff, though this amounted to weekly contact in no more than a quarter of cases. Many of the visits were for the purpose of capitalising on the concentration of resources and experience in the special school. Staff came to observe teaching techniques, study record keeping in individual learning programmes, and examine teaching materials and equipment. In a few cases they accompanied groups of pupils from an ordinary school to use the swimming pool in a special school.

LINKS AND SCHOOL MANAGEMENT

Link arrangements have major implications for the management of schools. Traditionally, schools have been seen as quite separate and independent of each other, and they have been managed accordingly. The head teacher is in sole command and is responsible for all the pupils in the school. All the staff working in the school are answerable to the head. Many ordinary schools have had to modify this concept of school management in order to build up provision for pupils with special needs, as various external specialists such as speech therapists, peripatetic teachers for the deaf and so on take responsibility for aspects of pupils' education but do not report to the head teacher of the school.

Link arrangements are set to modify this concept further in that they involve *pupils* attending a school who are not the responsibility of the head teacher of that school. This entails something that is qualitatively different from the above. A school is, like any other autonomous institution, a collection or system of components defined in part by its boundaries. The core components lie inside the boundaries – pupils and teachers, buildings, curriculum materials. Other elements that may have a great deal of impact on the school are, none the less, outside it – advisory services, parents, examination bodies, and other schools. If a boundary is repeatedly breached by a particular element that has been regarded as being on the other side, that boundary may have to be redrawn to include something previously excluded. Community schools are a case in point. In the past, schools regarded the local community as something external; as particular schools found ways of involving the community not just in supportive ways but in its core educational activities, new boundaries have had to be drawn that include elements of the community as integral features of the school. The net result is quite a different concept of what a school is about.

Link arrangements entail a similar shift in schools' conceptual boundaries and could lead to an even more radical revision of our concept of a school. If two schools are sharing pupils, teachers, and resources on a substantial basis, there is likely to be so much breaching of boundaries that the significance of the existing boundaries is called into question. There will be lots of anomalies in practice: pupils attending one school while on the roll of another, and also its responsibility; staff spending significant amounts of time working in a school without being responsible to the head teacher of that school; materials paid for out of one school's budget being used by another school.

It makes little sense in these situations to regard the partner schools, or attempt to manage them, as two totally separate institutions. The boundaries have to be redrawn, and new management units created. Goodwill and *ad hoc* arrangements may be all very well to begin with, but they will not suffice indefinitely. If a link arrangement is to have a durable and well-founded basis, the sharing of pupils and resources must be reflected in the management structure of the participant schools. This does not just mean sharing pupils but having joint responsibility for the curriculum, staffing, and resources. Appropriate staff in the partner schools must be given specific duties, for which they are jointly accountable, in respect of planning and maintaining the curriculum, allocating resources, and monitoring progress.

It must not be supposed that the shift in school management envisaged here will come about easily. Schools are jealous of their autonomy and are reluctant to engage in power sharing. There are, in any case, few precedents for school management structures of this kind, and appropriate models will have to be created rather than borrowed. Practical difficulties abound such as the disparity in size between large secondary schools and small special schools or the different relationships obtaining when a special school is linked with more than one ordinary school. None of this is reason for not seeking solutions. If link arrangements are not incorporated into agreed and workable management structures, they will turn out to be no more than a footnote in the history of provision for special educational needs and their potential for contributing to that provision will not be realised.

-10-

Training and professional development

NEW WINE, NEW BOTTLES

School reform on the scale envisaged here will not take place without a corresponding reform in training. If whole-school policies are to be implemented, with all the attendant implications for academic organisation, curriculum content, and teaching strategies, teachers must change – or be changed. Those who provide services, whether they be from Education, Health, or Social Services, must modify both the nature of their services and how they deliver them. Administrators too must adapt the ways in which they allocate the necessary resources.

All of this calls for attitude change and professional development on a major scale. Staff must believe that pupils should be educated alongside peers in as normal an environment as possible and that services should be shaped by pupil needs rather than the other way round. Teachers must recognise their responsibility for all children in their class and school catchment area and be committed to meeting their needs themselves without undue recourse to external agencies.

Benign attitudes are not sufficient on their own. The knowledge and skills traditionally associated with educating these pupils must be made more widely available. These can be drawn from the special schools, from remedial services, or from experienced teachers in ordinary schools. It will not all be relevant but a great deal of existing expertise can be utilised. In addition, because of the new approaches entailed by the concept of special educational need and the reforms implicit in whole-school provision, new knowledge and skills must be acquired and transmitted. Sayer (1985) points out the contradictions emerging, from the Warnock Report onward, when traditional forms of teacher support are grafted on to whole-school curriculum and management approaches. Finally, staff must learn to 'give away' their knowledge and skills. This requires the biggest attitude change of all. It entails engaging in consultancy, demystifying expertise, exercising skills systematically, and generally working in an open collaborative way.

How are these various changes to be brought about? Experience is a prime factor, especially where attitudes are concerned. Seeing what is possible and observing expert practitioners in action can be a major stimulus to change. Formal training is necessary to secure professional development in a systematic way. Such training must draw on a wide range of practice but must also set the lessons of experience into theoretical and other contexts. There is no one best way of providing the requisite training, and we shall see that there is currently a proliferation of training initiatives. The purpose of training is, of course, to enhance the education that pupils receive, and the most significant developments are those that translate training inputs into classroom practice.

This chapter maps the training provision currently available and notes some significant changes taking place in it. It begins with initial teacher training but is concerned mainly with inservice provision since this is where the main push must come. There is, in fact, a good deal of inservice innovation at all levels – national, local authority, and school. On-the-job learning is discussed, since it is an essential complement to formal training: the classroom is not only the arena where training is translated into practical action but also provides a valuable occasion of learning in its own right. Teachers are not the only staff concerned with improving ordinary school provision for pupils with special needs, and some training implications for other staff are noted. Finally, the notion of professional development as an integral part of professional practice is advanced, leading to a far broader concept of the school as a learning community.

INITIAL TRAINING

The starting point of any reform of teacher training must be initial training. Its potential for bringing about change may be modest but it does provide a backdrop against which other training must be viewed. It is also the platform on which future professional practice will be built. Two recent developments in initial training will be noted here: the move away from specialist training; and the growing inclusion of inputs on special needs.

Specialist initial training has never been a major feature of professional development in Britain, unlike the practice in several other countries where the separation between special schools and ordinary schools has been matched by a corresponding divide in the preparation of teachers. There have been a number of courses geared to the teaching of pupils with severe learning difficulties or to prepare teachers of the deaf. A report from the Advisory Council on the Supply and Education of Teachers (ACSET) in 1984 recommended that such courses should cease. Students in training should not specialise in special needs until they had completed general teacher training. All teachers should have a thorough grounding in mainstream teaching. Only after acquiring that – and ideally developing their skills in practice by a stint of actual teaching – should they specialise in teaching pupils with special needs.

The ACSET report proffers various reasons for making these changes – enhanced career opportunities for teachers, better use of the limited training resources, and so on. The most important reasons have to do with the twin principles of integration and meeting pupils' needs. If schools are to regard the provision made for pupils with special needs as an integral part of the whole school's educational provision, staff must have a common base of training. Specialist expertise is not to be discounted, but it must come to the greatest extent possible from fellow teachers and not from separate experts, whether they be members of external services or colleague teachers with totally different training.

There have been some misgivings about these proposals. Particular concern has been expressed over the possible dilution of expertise and scarce training resources. The changes are going ahead however. It is clear that the alternative arrangements proposed for providing specialist training later in teachers' careers must be implemented and that inservice training generally must be expanded if pupils' need of specialist teaching is to be met.

A second noteworthy development in initial teacher training is the greater attention being paid to special educational needs. Some pre-service courses have long had inputs on special needs in one form or another. These were not sufficiently widespread however and, in any case, were often optional. The Warnock Report quotes evidence from Scotland indicating that a majority of primary teachers felt inadequately prepared for teaching slow learners. A similar picture emerges from other more recent sources such as Croll and Moses (1985).

The Warnock Report recommended that all courses of initial teacher training, including those leading to a postgraduate certificate in education, should have a 'special education element'. This should aim to:

- develop an awareness that all teachers are likely to be concerned with pupils who have special educational needs
- enable teachers to recognise early signs of possible difficulties

- give teachers knowledge of the part they can play in assessing and meeting special needs
- give teachers knowledge of what special educational provision is like
- provide some acquaintance with special schools, special classes and units
- make teachers aware of the importance of working with parents and develop the skills to communicate effectively with them
- above all, give teachers knowledge in general terms of when and where to refer for special help. (12.7)

The Report went on to outline the range of skills, understanding and appreciation that must be developed if these aims are to be achieved.

The ACSET Report (1984) also laid down some requirements for all teachers that would have to be met in initial teacher training. Thus, all teachers 'need to know how to identify the special educational needs of children and young people, what they need to do themselves to meet those needs and when and how to enlist specialist help'. The Council for the Accreditation of Teacher Education (CATE) gave these proposals bite with its stipulation that proposals for initial training courses *had* to include coverage of special educational needs, on a compulsory as opposed to an optional basis.

> Students should be introduced to ways of identifying children with special educational needs, helped to appreciate what the ordinary school can and cannot do for such children and given some knowledge of the specialist help available and how it can be enlisted.
> (Annex, para 11 in DES, 1984a)

If the coverage was not satisfactory, course approval could be withheld.

It is not going to be easy for training institutions to respond fully to these demands. Many lack the requisite expertise. All have the problem of finding the time, especially on the one year postgraduate courses. Special needs is just one of many components jostling for space in overcrowded programmes. Even if the Warnock expedient of locating the special needs input 'within the general context of child development' (12.10) were adopted, existing training time-tables allow little leeway. Thomas and Smith (1985) give a good idea of the practical difficulties. They also discuss the pros and cons of different approaches – whether the special needs input should be self-contained or integrated into training programmes as a whole; what mixture of general awareness and specific skills it should comprise; and what the balance should be between lectures/seminars and school-based experience.

If the concept of special educational need is taken seriously and schools' part in creating learning difficulties is acknowledged, there can be little doubt but that the special needs input to initial teacher training must permeate the whole course. Specific contributions on particular disabilities or teaching techniques may be presented in a self-contained way. If the teaching is to have impact, however, it must make teachers aware of the need to match class teaching and school structures to the learning situation of all pupils and enable them to do so in practice.

As to the balance between general awareness and specific skills, there is growing consensus in favour of the latter. Smith (1983) found that students who had done courses containing both types of component regarded the practical skills element more useful. They particularly valued teaching practice with groups of slow learners. Gulliford (1986) considered that the Warnock outline probably gave too much emphasis to building up awareness and knowledge of a general kind. More attention needed to be paid to skills and to the kind of knowledge related to practical issues in teaching.

INSERVICE TRAINING

Welcome and necessary though these changes in initial training are, they will not on their own effect much change in the short term. Initial training is at the edge of the problem and in this context is best seen as an investment for the future. Teachers in schools have already been trained! Most serving teachers for many years to come will not be affected by current innovations in initial training. It is, moreover, precisely those teachers who are long-serving and experienced who occupy the positions of leadership in schools. They take the crucial decisions on the curriculum and academic organisation of the school, and effectively control the progress of any school reform. For this reason, inservice training is centrally important and is probably the most important single factor in determining the extent to which effective reform will take place.

There are at least two further contexts in which inservice training should be considered, one quite general and one specific to the special needs area. The first has to do with the growing awareness of the importance of regular training throughout one's professional life. This is partly to update skills and keep abreast of new developments but it also has to do with developing in a professional role. Quite simply, not everything can be taught at the outset before a person has experience of doing the job. Depth of understanding comes with experience, and skill mastery is acquired with practice. Much is learnt from actually doing the job, but the point of regular training inputs is to facilitate this learning and to ensure that it is relevant and enhances the individual's professional contribution. Without it the individual runs the risk of being locked into self-regarding idiosyncracy. Such professional development is increasingly seen as an essential part of the experience of all teachers, and inservice training for special needs work is simply taking its place alongside similar training in mathematics, foreign languages, and other aspects of school work.

Secondly, as noted in chapter 5, special schools have been regarded as an important source of training in special needs. Some would argue that they provide the ideal setting for new entrants to the profession and ensure that they receive a comprehensive and practical grounding in the skills required. They can learn from more experienced colleagues and can see at first hand the great variety of learning difficulties that children have. To the extent that this actually happens – and by no means all special schools have the expertise or provide the creative milieu that fosters professional development – any move away from special schooling toward integration will lead to a training gap. This gap must necessarily be filled by inservice training.

How are teachers in ordinary schools to receive the inservice training that teaching pupils with special educational needs requires? The range of practice is enormous and can only be outlined here. It can be categorised in various ways – the content of courses, mode of delivery, duration, target group, and so on. What will be offered here is a description of courses in terms of the location of responsibility for them: training institution, local education authority, and other.

Training institutions

The training institutions – universities, polytechnics, and colleges of higher education – are a major source of formal inservice training. Four types of training can be distinguished.

1. Extended postgraduate study. This is normally at master's or doctorate level. It is carried out on a full-time or part-time basis and can extend from one to five or more years. Doctoral study is geared to doing original research. Master's programmes can also consist of research, sometimes transferring to a doctorate, or they can be based on a substantial amount of lectures and course work. Study at this level tends to be regarded as rather academic and, despite the growing focus on practical projects, to be somewhat removed from the classroom. It is still relatively uncommon and constitutes a small part of the overall pattern of inservice provision. The associated qualifications are very far from achieving the currency that they have in places like the United States.

2. *One-year full-time courses or their equivalent.* These courses usually lead to the award of a Diploma in Special Educational Needs. There are more than 70 such courses in England and Wales spread across 46 training institutions. Comparable courses, planned on a national basis, have recently been developed in Scotland. These courses are described in more detail below.

3. *One-term courses.* 1983 saw a major innovation in inservice training that has changed the pattern of provision for good. Circular 3/83 introduced a system of direct grants to local authorities in partial replacement of the old 'pooling' arrangements to fund inservice training in particular topics. Special Educational Needs in Ordinary Schools was one of the initial priority areas and has remained as such in the intervening period. This has led to the development of a considerable number of courses of one term's duration, intended for teachers who have responsibilities for pupils with special educational needs in primary and secondary schools. The courses are discussed in more detail below.

4. *Open University course – 'Special needs in education'.* Like other Open University courses, this is based on distance learning; students receive written material and audio cassettes by post, most specially produced for the course, and watch television broadcasts (generally at unsocial hours!). They can attend occasional tutorials in their own locality, run by the course tutor who marks their assignments. The course runs for a year and is designated a half-credit course. (In theory, two credits correspond to a year's full-time work; in practice, the course is the equivalent of rather more than one term's work.) For 1987, the course can count toward the award of a modular diploma.

The course is organised round four main themes: (i) understanding special education; (ii) meeting special needs; (iii) relating special education to the education system as a whole; and (iv) integrating pupils with special needs into ordinary schools. These are covered through 16 specially written units, eight television programmes, and eight audio presentations, along with a great deal of supplementary material and selected reading lists.

The course is not restricted to teachers or those professionally involved with pupils who have special educational needs. It is 'for everyone who is interested in the education of children with disabilities and other difficulties... for those who wish to move towards an education system that meets the needs of all children' (Open University, 1985). Whilst the majority of the thousand plus who take the course each year are teachers, a significant number of other people, including parents, have taken it as well. Some local authorities make group bookings for the course each year and build on it to provide inservice training relevant to local needs.

Local education authorities

Local authorities are playing an increasing part in inservice provision. Not only are they tending to specify their requirements rather more and collaborate with the training institutions in the actual delivery of courses, but some are setting up their own inservice programmes as well. These are generally short programmes, organised and run by local authority staff. A particular focus of such training has been to equip teachers in ordinary schools to recognise and teach pupils with special educational needs. Hegarty and Pocklington (1981) and Wolfendale (1987) give examples of such programmnes, which range from termly 'professional development' days for the staff of special classes and units and week-long general awareness courses for all teachers to quite substantial courses on identifying and meeting special needs.

One of the best known and most comprehensive local authority training initiatives is the Special Needs Action Programme (SNAP) developed in Coventry in the early eighties. It has led to the production of considerable amounts of training materials, books, manuals, tape/slide presentations, and videos. These are commercially available and have been widely taken up. The course organisers in Coventry estimate that over half the education authorities in the country are using at least some of these materials.

Muncey and Ainscow (1983) describe the Programme in detail and outline its early development; Moses (1987) reports on an evaluation designed to measure its continuing impact. The Programme is focussed on primary schools and aims to help teachers to develop identification procedures, provide an appropriate curriculum, and co-ordinate the work of the support agencies. Materials have been prepared on such topics as learning difficulties in the primary school, daily measurement, developing individualised programmes, hearing difficulties, visual difficulties, emotional and behavioural problems. A version of the Programme suitable for use in secondary schools is under preparation.

The key to the Programme is a three-part pyramid structure. The original need was to make an impact in a large number of schools in a short space of time and to do so in such a way as to achieve lasting change. These are, of course, the major challenges facing any form of inservice training. The first step in responding to them was to bring head teachers together to introduce the Programme and the thinking behind it and to explain what participation in it would entail. Each school appointed a co-ordinator who attended six sessions, comprising small group discussions and workshop activities, in order to work through the specific content. The co-ordinators then organised follow-up activities back in their own schools, in accordance with a school-based policy for pupils with special needs and drawing on support from the local authority.

The Programme has achieved a considerable degree of success. It has been fully implemented in Coventry and the level of take-up elsewhere indicates a positive endorsement of the materials by professional colleagues. The evaluation in Coventry by Moses indicated that all the co-ordinators found the course a rewarding and enjoyable experience. They felt that its content and methods had been appropriate and that it had equipped them to take on the role of co-ordinator in their schools. A considerable amount of follow-up training activity had been arranged in schools, and all schools showed a high level of concern about the identification and subsequent teaching of pupils with difficulties.

Other arrangements

Inservice training is provided in a variety of other ways. Three sources in particular will be picked out: (i) joint arrangements between local authorities and training institutions; (ii) school initiatives; and (iii) assorted bodies.

The training offered by local authorities and training institutions respectively has been described so far as if they were entirely separate from each other. In the past they tended to operate independently, and still do to a certain extent, but the barriers are coming down. This is evident in the one-term courses described above and in the Open University course 'Special needs in education'; local authorities are telling the training institutions what they want from inservice courses or adapting the training packages produced to fit their own requirements. It is evident, too, in the training initiatives taken by education authorities who draw on the expertise of local training institutions.

This trend is likely to become more pronounced in the wake of recent changes in government policy on inservice provision – changes that are backed by a significant shift in the pattern of funding. Details are given in Circular 6/86 (DES, 1986a). The pooling arrangements for funding local authority inservice training are to be discontinued. Authorities will instead receive an individual allocation directly from the Department of Education and Science. This will be based on a proposal submitted by the authority setting out its training plans. Such proposals should take account both of locally assessed training needs and of national priorities as determined by the government. Training for special needs naturally falls within these arrangements.

The effect of this is to give local authorities far greater responsibility for inservice training than most have hitherto exercised. It also fundamentally alters the relationship between them and the training institutions. The authorities are now the customers, who will only buy – or can afford to buy – certain products. The training institutions must adapt themselves to supply these products if they are to stay in business. Ideally, the two parties will come together and work out training strategies and provision jointly, as has begun to happen with the one-term courses. It is also strongly encouraged in the Circular. When such joint planning does take place, training can be geared to actual service needs and fit into a considered local strategy but can also capitalise on formal training expertise and benefit from experience in other localities.

A second source of training is that arranged by schools, either on their own or in consortium with neighbouring schools or other agencies. Such school-based training is, by its very nature, highly specific to the local situation. It is often limited in the resources it can call upon and runs a risk of being parochial and inward-looking. It is, however, a low cost way of promoting staff development at local level and, properly run, can be a highly effective way of communicating a set of messages to all the staff, both teaching and non-teaching, of a school. It can also complement external training by identifying gaps where a school needs an injection of training, helping staff who have been away on courses to translate what they have learnt into relevant action in the school and disseminating to the entire staff what individuals have learnt.

Hodgson, Clunies-Ross and Hegarty (1984) describe a number of school-based courses that grew out of internal discussion about staff needs and development. Most of them took place out of school hours and were generally bound by local constraints. They do, however, demonstrate the scope for tapping the expertise available at local level. The potential for school-based training is enhanced when schools work together. This is particularly so in the case of the link arrangements between special schools and ordinary schools described in the previous chapter. Staff have complementary skills and experience and can share them by means of training courses or other ways. Hallmark and Dessent (1982) describe one programme of support offered by a special school to neighbouring primary schools: the purpose was to equip teachers with the skills to identify pupils' needs and to devise and implement appropriate learning programmes.

Finally, training can come from a variety of other sources – both official agencies and voluntary bodies. Her Majesty's Inspectorate arrange short courses, usually residential and lasting about a week, for teachers and others working in the education service; their general purpose is to stimulate new thinking and approaches in a way that will encourage participants to arrange further dissemination in their own localities. The Special Education Microelectronics Resource Centres hold short courses on aspects of the new information technologies and how they can be used in the education of pupils with special needs. There are numerous courses run by voluntary bodies, notably the Spastics Society, which has its own training centre in Oxfordshire; many of its courses are rather specialised, but some are relevant to staff in ordinary schools. Other bodies running relevant courses include the National Association for Remedial Education, the National Council for Special Education, the Association for All Speech Impaired Children, and the British Institute for Mental Handicap.

ONE-YEAR DIPLOMA COURSES

The ACSET report referred to above stated that local education authorities need to employ 'specialist teachers who between them have detailed knowledge of the spectrum of special educational needs and the responses required'. Such teachers should, after acquiring a firm foundation of experience of teaching in ordinary schools, have undertaken the equivalent of one year's study leading to a recognised qualification. This could be done on the basis of a full-time secondment or through a flexible part-time commitment. The one-year training courses should provide:

> a common core of knowledge and competencies for participants which enables them to understand how special educational needs may arise from interacting factors in the child, the family, school and the community

and

> the opportunity for individuals to develop a specialization in the needs of certain groups of pupils, such as those with emotional and behavioural disorders, or under fives with special educational needs.
> (ACSET, para 10)

These courses will play a key part in the future development of special needs provision, and the NFER accordingly mounted a study of the courses running in England and Wales in 1984/85. Summary findings are given in Dust and Moses (1986). Of the 74 courses, exactly half were full-time and half part-time. Most of the part-time courses ran for two years, though one modular course could extend up to six years. The content of courses was exceedingly diverse. Just one-fifth of the courses (15) dealt with a single area of special educational need, spanning severe learning difficulties, emotional and behavioural difficulties, mild and moderate learning difficulties, hearing impairment, visual impairment, and specific learning difficulties. The remaining 59 courses were either generic, covering the whole range of special needs, or concentrated on two or three areas of special need.

Students on the courses were split fairly evenly between the special school and the ordinary school sector. Most were in relatively junior positions; more than three-quarters were on scale 1 or 2. The courses generally had an entry prerequisite of two or three years' teaching experience; in the event, most students had had substantial teaching experience.

Assessment for certification was based on a variable mixture of coursework, dissertation, written examination, and oral examination. The most frequent combination of assessment methods was coursework and dissertation. All courses required students to submit coursework – usually based on a detailed child study or other practical activity – as part of the assessment procedure. Most required a dissertation as well; this had to be a substantial piece of work – 10,000 words was common – and would ideally combine theory and practice. Less than one-third of courses used written examinations. Oral examinations were relatively uncommon, in some cases being used only for borderline candidates.

Two courses in particular are noteworthy for their innovative features. The first is a two-year part-time course on visual handicap offered by the University of Birmingham (Chapman, 1982). This runs alongside the full-time course but is available on a distance learning basis. Appropriate learning materials to cover the course content have been prepared and arrangements are made for assessing students on teaching practice. This mode of course delivery seems particularly suited to a situation where the number of teachers applying for training is small and they are spread around the country.

The second is a modular course offered through a range of institutions in the north-west of England (Robson, 1984). There is a wide choice of modules, or learning units, that can be studied in different settings. Students select their own programme of study within a coherent framework; this ensures balance as well as professional relevance. Study is part-time and flexibly arranged to suit teachers' requirements, subject to a minimum of two years and a maximum of six. The course is validated both by the University of Manchester and Manchester Polytechnic. It has been evaluated as part of a DES-funded study of inservice provision (Robson, et al., 1987).

A national programme of inservice training based on one-year diplomas has been developed in Scotland in recent years. Blythman (1985) describes the planning and extensive consultation that went into this. An earlier Inspectorate report pin-pointed the need for major curriculum reform in schools (Scottish Education Department, 1978). The debate that followed led to a consensus that new forms of inservice training were required that would prepare remedial specialists, particularly in respect of consultancy and co-operative teaching.

A national committee representing the different interest groups proposed a new advanced diploma and laid down General Requirements to guide specific course proposals from the training institutions. The Requirements, which are a model of clarity, outline the knowledge, skills, and attitudes to be encompassed, course structure and administration, selection of students, and assessment procedures. The first courses were running in 1982, and within two years courses had been established in most of the Scottish colleges of education. The courses are quite diverse, in response to local priorities and constraints, but – unlike the situation obtaining in England and Wales – they do fit into a common framework.

Finally, there is the new Open University Advanced Diploma in Special Needs in Education. This is a modular course offered for the first time in 1987. It is designed to assist teachers in preventing or reducing the learning difficulties encountered by pupils in all curriculum areas.

The Diploma is in two parts and can be studied in a minimum of two years. The first part comprises the course 'Special needs in education' described above and one other course chosen from a list of compatible Open University courses. The second part is based on a single course 'Applied studies in learning difficulties in education'. This course is constructed round the execution of three projects under the general headings of (i) pupil learning, (ii) curriculum development, and (iii) decision making and policy.

ONE-TERM COURSES

One-term courses are a major innovation in inservice training provision. They represent a move by the government to establish priorities and to direct expenditure on training. The purpose is to encourage local authorities to release teachers for training in designated priority areas. The scheme operates by carefully targetted financing: if local authorities send teachers for training in a designated area, they can recover the cost of employing replacement teachers from central funds.

Special Educational Needs in Ordinary Schools was one of five priority areas designated in 1983. Priority areas are designated annually, and it has continued to feature each year since then. Relevant courses should be for one term on a full-time basis or a sandwich pattern equivalent. Circular 3/85 specifies that they are intended for 'teachers who have, or may be taking up, responsibility for children with special educational needs in primary or secondary schools'. They should assist teachers in

> (1) identifying and devising strategies to overcome impediments to pupils' learning;
> (2) considering the implications, for the curriculum of the school as a whole, of the presence of children with a range of special educational needs; and
> (3) implementing forms of appropriate organisation for additional and supplementary help which will give such children access to the full range of the curriculum.
>
> (DES, 1985b)

NFER made a study of the 25 one-term courses in operation over the period 1984/85. Questionnaire data were obtained from the institutions of higher education providing courses. More detailed information was collected by interview from three course providers. Interviews were also held with a sample of course members and local authority co-ordinators. The result was a detailed account of the courses from the perspectives of the training institutions, the local authorities, the teachers and their schools. Details are given in Moses and Hegarty (1988).

Two features of the courses stand out: the deliberate effort to bring about change in course members' schools; and the close links between local authorities and the training institutions.

The underlying emphasis throughout the courses was one of equipping teachers to develop aspects of their schools' provision for pupils with special educational needs. There were four main elements of the courses:

1. Core taught component, giving students an up-to-date understanding of special educational needs and how ordinary schools can respond, and equipping them with some of the necessary skills.
2. Professional visits and attachments.

3. Introduction to the work of the advisory and support service, with particular reference to course members' own authorities and where they can turn to for help.
4. School project.

The school project was a key element and in most courses was allocated a substantial amount of time – one to two days a week. The aim of the project was to develop an aspect of provision for pupils with special needs in the course member's own school. The focus of the project was decided before the course started, in agreement with the head teacher, the local authority co-ordinator, and the course tutor. Time was spent on the course assembling the requisite information to draw up a detailed plan for implementation in the school after the course was over. Topics chosen covered a wide span – developing record-keeping procedures, using a support teacher, devising individualised programmes of learning, developing parti-cular areas of the curriculum, setting up a whole-school approach to special needs, promoting parental involvement. The time spent by the teacher on the course was, in essence, an opportunity to engage in detailed, reflective planning and acquire any resources that might be needed subsequently. Whilst not all projects were successful, many were taken forward and seemed likely to result in lasting change in their schools.

Local authorities played a greater part in these courses than is customary with externally provided training. Each appointed a co-ordinator, usually a special needs adviser, to liaise with the training institution and be generally responsible for the authority's students on the course. The authorities' involvement with courses encompassed planning, teaching, and feedback. Because of the unusual nature of the courses, the training institutions set up planning groups composed of course tutors and local authority personnel. This gave the opportunity for service perspectives to be represented and for specific teaching inputs from the local authorities to be planned. In some cases the planning group continued to meet after the initial planning task was done. This was to exchange perspectives between the training institutions and the authorities on a regular basis, discuss matters such as the selection procedures for candidates, and generally to monitor progress and ensure that the course was on target.

The local authority input to teaching was variable, averaging between ten and twenty per cent of lecture time, but significant. All courses had some outside contributors. In one case the course was taught almost exclusively by local authority personnel, with the college tutor playing a co-ordinating role. The major contribution from authority staff was on the work of the advisory and support services. There was some input on psychologists' reports and how to interpret them. Local authorities also helped in arranging visits to schools.

As far as course members were concerned, local authority staff selected teachers for the courses and supported them subsequently. The training institutions issued guidelines about the course but selection of candidates lay in the hands of the authorities. Some had a long-term plan to build up expertise in special needs across the authority's schools in a coherent way and geared their selection procedures accordingly. Most local authority co-ordinators arranged meetings with candidates before they started the course. Some kept in touch while they were on the course and assisted them in the follow-up work back at their schools when it was over.

ON-THE-JOB LEARNING

On-the-job learning has a long and honourable history. For centuries apprentices have sat at the feet of masters, gradually working up from simple skills to more complex. As noted above, special schools see it as one of their strengths that they can provide the kind of training environment where newcomers to the field can learn from their colleagues. Ordinary schools are not conducive to such learning: many teachers operate in isolation from colleagues, often behind closed doors, and there is little opportunity for sharing skills.

What is necessary is that ordinary schools create the kind of milieu where this sharing can happen. Hegarty and Pocklington (1981) identified a number of ways in which schools were attempting to do this. They gave practical examples to illustrate each different one.

Instruction. Some specialists adopted a formal role of instructing their colleagues or developing their skills and understanding in other, relatively formal ways. Such instruction was directed at both teachers and classroom assistants. Teachers, for instance, benefited from being shown how to assess a pupil's learning difficulties and draw up an appropriate teaching programme and from seeing how particular pupils were handled by more experienced colleagues. Classroom assistants picked up a good deal from watching teachers and therapists at work, but could learn far more if the latter formally instructed them. A speech therapist, for example, who could only visit a school at intervals involved a classroom assistant in the work by having her sit in on therapy sessions, explaining what she was doing and why; then she had the assistant take the lesson, working to her instructions and in her presence so that she could correct and amplify as necessary. In this way, the ancillary gained confidence in carrying out specific speech therapy exercises and in time took the majority of sessions on her own.

Joint working. Collaboration on common tasks can be a valuable source of professional development. The examples given by Hegarty and Pocklington refer to curriculum development but the training benefits can be realised in almost any area of work. Focussed discussion on matters of professional concern is rare enough in teaching. What joint working does is to facilitate such discussion and promote staff development through communal reflection – working through common problems, evaluating different solutions, and generally broadening individuals' perspectives on their shared professional tasks.

Team teaching. Team teaching is an arrangement whereby two or more teachers pool their classes or resources and plan educational activities in a flexible way for the group as a whole. It is a particular form of joint working. It is not peculiar to special education, but it does offer significant advantages in the education of pupils with special needs in the ordinary school. Not least amongst these are the training benefits that can accrue. Team teaching forces teachers into more conscious planning, detailing objectives and spelling out teaching methods and resources to be used. It provides the all too rare opportunity to observe colleagues' teaching – and to have one's own teaching observed and commented on. As with other forms of joint working, it leads teachers to have focussed professional conversation on individual pupils. Where one of the team has a particular background in special needs, these training benefits are more likely to be achieved.

Contact with experts. Access to people with expert knowledge and developed skills can lead to specific professional development. Such access is particularly important when teachers have only intermittent contact with pupils with special needs. A teacher who has a hearing impaired pupil for a few periods a week over one year may not want to become an expert on hearing impairment but does need ready access to an expert throughout the year. When this access takes the form of being able to observe the professional at work the potential for professional development is clear. Teachers gain a deeper understanding of children's learning difficulties and how to handle them. Seeing a psychologist or speech therapist at work gives teachers a clearer perspective on assessment and its implications or on speech therapy skills and how they might be integrated into classroom work. There are major benefits too for classroom assistants from being in the classroom. Observing what teachers do, the way they relate to pupils, how they handle different situations, the learning activities set up – all of this is crucial in equipping them to move beyond the traditional, rather limited role of the classroom assistant to making a more independent skill-based contribution to the education of pupils with special needs.

Visits and meetings. The opportunity to see at first hand what is happening in other schools is too seldom available to teachers. This can be particularly important for staff concerned with special needs in ordinary schools, since often they are few in number and their combined experience is relatively limited. Ironically, the fact that specialist staff are few in number can make it more difficult for them to get out of school for visits or to go on courses. The opportunity to visit is especially useful when new provision is being set up or major changes made in existing provision. Staff can see a variety of approaches that others have adopted and gather ideas for practice in their own school. Even if there is nothing that can be copied directly it is still useful to examine the concrete details of an actual provision, find out why things have been done as they are, and discuss problems and prospects with the staff running it. Meetings with colleagues from other schools, whilst not having the direct impact of visits, also help in broadening individuals' perspectives.

EXTERNAL STAFF

Whilst the primary concern here is with teachers, there is a range of other staff to be kept in mind – advisers, peripatetic and advisory teachers, educational psychologists, speech therapists, physiother-apists, and medical officers. They have a significant contribution to make to the education of pupils with special needs, and it is essential that they make this contribution whether pupils attend special schools or ordinary schools.

It has to be assumed here that these various staff are properly trained in the professional content of their own work – that the psychologist is competent in the practice of assessment, that the speech therapist knows how to diagnose language problems and devise appropriate remediation programmes, that the peripatetic specialist is versed in teaching pupils with visual impairment, and so on. Something more than these core professional skills is required however. New skills – and new attitudes toward the deployment of expertise – must be brought into play. Two underlying themes run through this: the educational context of ordinary schooling; and the need to share skills.

Some of the professionals in question are well aware of the ordinary school context. Others, especially those from health and social services backgrounds, are less familiar with schools. Pupils with special needs must be seen primarily from an *educational* perspective as far as ordinary schools are concerned. Some conditions require specific medical or therapeutic interventions, which can be provided without reference to the school. Interventions made by these professionals, however, should be set in a context of enhancing the education that pupils receive. To do this effectively, the professionals must be aware of the educational implications of pupils' handicapping conditions and have some knowledge of what goes on in schools. The medical officer must realise that there is not a direct link between physical condition and educational need, and that two children with identical physical difficulties may need very different educational programmes. If a physiotherapist wants to integrate particular movement exercises into a pupil's daily routine, he or she must know how the pupil spends the day. A psychologist who wants to translate the information obtained from assessment into practical teaching action must be aware of the constraints surrounding the teacher in the classroom.

The various professionals need to extend their perspectives on disability so that they do not lose sight of the educational context. They must also find ways of translating the specific insights that *their* specialism yields into practical action that is feasible for the ordinary school. Special schools may have facilitated this with their concentration of pupils with special needs and the more intensive involvement that professionals have with them. If professionals' contact is only with individual pupils dispersed across different ordinary schools, appropriate inservice training is likely to add greatly to their effectiveness.

The second area in which the outside professionals may need some training has to do with the exchange of relevant skills. This is not a question of enabling the teacher or the classroom assistant to do the professional's job but rather of enriching the former's set of competences and helping to compensate for the scarcity of the professional's time. In order to do this, professionals need to develop appropriate attitudes toward their own role and toward colleagues; they must also acquire certain second-order skills to do with exercise of their basic professional skills.

The attitudes required have to do with openess and collaboration, with willingness to share skills and readiness to learn from others, with commitment to dialogue and shared activities. They are the antithesis of clinging to professional mystiques and lines of demarcation. Some professionals have a precious view of their specialism and display little regard for the insights and procedures associated with other specialisms. This kind of thinking is clearly hostile to what is being proposed here. The different professionals must learn to see their specialism in perspective. They have to refrain from 'hijacking' a child's difficulties and insisting that their account of them is the one that really matters. Any given specialism can only offer a partial, albeit unique perspective, and it is incumbent upon the different specialists to develop a collaborative stance whereby insights from different backgrounds are woven together to give a fuller account of a child's learning difficulties.

This attitude is operationalised in various ways. It can mean, for instance, being prepared to exercise one's skills in front of others. Psychologists doing assessments have tended to withdraw children to a secluded place – rather as if they were doing a medical examination. The same is often true of speech therapists running a therapy session. Sometimes there are good reasons for this isolation but not always. If professionals want to demystify their skills they must be willing to work in front of teachers, classroom assistants, and parents as appropriate. They must also be ready to explain what they are about, both to elucidate their procedures and to help interpret the outcomes.

Collaborative attitudes are not enough on their own of course; they have to be backed up with appropriate skills. Competence in a professional skill does not necessarily equip one to communicate it. This holds true whether the aim is to instruct others in the skill or to explain the outcomes to them. The latter is particularly difficult because of the translation task involved. Professionals use technical terms, so-called jargon, as a convenient and precise shorthand; these are generally based on a body of theoretical knowledge and it can be very difficult to paraphrase them into everyday language without distortion or loss of precision.

The need then is for training in these second-order skills. The professional has to learn to stand back from his or her role and look at it reflectively. Skills of explaining and communicating, of working collaboratively as part of a team, must be acquired. When this has been done, the outside professionals will truly be in a position to contribute to the education of pupils with special needs in ordinary schools.

THE SCHOOL AS A LEARNING COMMUNITY

There is much to welcome in recent developments in the training of teachers. Initial training is being revitalised and made more relevant to the work of the classroom, and a rich pattern of inservice provision is emerging. Greater attention is being paid to special educational needs in initial training. In the best practice this permeates the whole course, so that teaching pupils with special educational needs is not seen as a remote and separate activity but as an aspect of teaching that has some special features. The diversity of inservice provision at national, local authority, and school levels has been described. Politicians and professionals alike see it as the way to meet the staff development needs of the system and there is growing encouragement to teachers to avail themselves of inservice opportunities. Many of these opportunities feature special educational needs, either as a major element in its own right or as an aspect of other topics.

There is still a great deal to be done, not least if all training is to match the level of the best current practice, but progress is being made and seems likely to continue. The focus on inservice training is a particular strength of the new arrangements. It is widely recognised in most walks of life that initial training does no more than begin the work of professional training. For teachers, it should equip them to start work in the classroom but, as important, it should lay the foundations for subsequent professional development. This is where inservice training must play a key part and also why it is so important for local authorities and schools to have staff development policies which translate into action for all staff.

There is one further step, perhaps the most important of all. This is for each school to take responsibility for the professional development of its own staff. Just as in the case of pupils and their learning needs, staff must be helped to identify their professional development needs and give assistance in meeting them. Training provided by external agencies can only go part of the way here. No matter how well training institutions and local authorities collaborate, or how relevant to practice the courses on offer, they can do no more than provide a framework of opportunity.

Whether or not anything is built on this framework depends on the school. The key factor is how schools regard professional development: an optional extra to be taken up when job pressures permit, or an integral feature of doing the job properly. Too often schools see it as the former, and miss out on the opportunities created by the fact that they are institutions of learning and that teachers have daily contact with young people learning. Too often the only learning that is done is by pupils. Teachers too should be learning – from each other, from their pupils and from reflective scrutiny of their work. When this happens schools will become real learning communities, where professional development is an integral part of professional practice and where pupil learning and teacher learning reinforce each other.

A role for parents

RIGHTS AND RHETORIC

Parents have come a long way in the education system over the past 20 years. From being a tiresome necessity and at best an adjunct to the work of schools, they have become partners and key contributors. The Plowden Report posited in 1967 that 'one of the essentials for educational advance is a closer partnership between the two parties to every child's education'. The Warnock Report in 1978 regarded the parents of children with special educational needs as 'equal partners in the educational process'; so important was this fact that on its recognition depended the success of its wide-ranging proposals for reform. In 1985 the White Paper *Better Schools* considered that 'parent and school become partners in a shared task for the benefit of the child'.

There is clearly no shortage of rhetoric in favour of parents as partners in the educational process. Welcome though these statements are, it is well to note their recency and realise that official pronouncements are often well ahead of everyday practice and attitudes. Schools have traditionally kept parents at arms length. When they lowered the barriers it was often to instruct parents with a view to the physical and moral welfare of their children. Sometimes it was the parents who kept their distance. This is exemplified by the long-standing traditions of the independent school sector, where boarding schools in particular have been expected to get on with their task of turning out suitably socialised young men and women without bothering the parents, save in the case of very serious disciplinary matters. These attitudes are far from extinct. There are many in schools who regard parental involvement as an unwelcome intrusion promoted by misguided do-gooders; just as some parents –from all sections of society – are more than happy for schools to take over responsibility for their children's education. To overlook these facts is to risk being washed away by the growing waves of enthusiasm and official rhetoric regarding parental involvement in schooling.

A rationale for involving parents in their children's schooling comes from the acknowledged importance of the home environment and from the right of parents to have an influence on educational matters. A great deal is known about child development and the major role that parents play. Regardless of the relative contributions of heredity and environment, it is not disputed that children from favoured environments derive educational benefits from those environments, whereas children from disadvantaged backgrounds suffer a consequent educational loss.

Parents' formal and legal rights in education have received growing acknowledgement in recent years. As well as the reports mentioned above, the Taylor Report in 1977 spelled out parents' rights to know what is going on in their child's school and to have a greater say in running it. The Education Act 1980 gave parents new rights in choosing schools and in receiving information about them, whilst the Education Act 1981 established the right of parents to be consulted on matters relating to the assessment and placement of their children with special educational needs. In addition to these relatively formal rights, it is widely held that parents are entitled to a far greater degree of participation in the work and management of schools than is currently common.

Where home–school links exist, the outstanding feature is the diversity of practice. Parental involvement projects have been set up for many reasons and exhibit a corresponding variety of objectives and approaches. They range from highly structured home teaching programmes, such as Portage, to school-based drop-in facilities for parents, from local authority schemes to initiatives taken by individual class teachers.

Developments in the area have been reviewed by Wolfendale (1983) and Mortimore and Mortimore (1984). The latter group the different schemes under four headings, according to their main function: (i) intervening in early learning and mother–child interaction, with a focus on enrichment; (ii) easing the transition from home to pre-school or school; (iii) developing parental involvement programmes in schools; and (iv) involving parents in their children's learning at home, in particular by hearing them read.

Wolfendale concentrates on primary schools and describes a number of initiatives. These are located within a framework which is elaborated in Wolfendale (1987) (in the present series). There are two main groupings depending on whether the direction of influence is from parents to school or from school to home. In the first group, the activities may be (i) concrete and practical, e.g., fund raising, (ii) pedagogical, e.g., parents contributing to curriculum planning or to teaching, (iii) focussed on policy and governing, or (iv) communal activities for parents and children. The second group – school to home – entails schools (i) giving information to parents,

(ii) providing support, (iii) giving instruction, or (iv) making input to the rest of the community. Some of the initiatives described involve the parents of children with special educational needs.

Much of the literature on working with these parents comes from the special school sector. The original impetus in the United Kingdom came from teachers of the hearing impaired who worked on a 'parent guidance' model. In recent years teachers of pupils with severe learning difficulties have sought close collaboration with parents. There is little evidence of effective partnership involving teachers of other groups of pupils. Mittler and Mittler (1982) in a useful review proposed a rationale for partnership and developed the implications for practice in a concrete way.

The challenge now is to weave the two strands of mainstream and special school initiatives together. There are specific techniques and practice from the special school sector that could usefully be adapted for use in ordinary schools. Equally, the collaboration of ordinary schools with parents of children with special needs must take account of the more general developments in home-school partnership. If it does not fit within the emerging framework of such a partnership, the likelihood is that it will isolate pupils with special educational needs and block their participation in the life of the school.

This chapter considers what is entailed in this partnership and outlines some of the key functions that it serves. This is followed by a discussion of attitudes: Do parents of children with special educational needs actually want their children to go to ordinary schools, and do they wish to be involved in the work of the school? Finally, some practical suggestions for promoting parental involvement are advanced.

DIMENSIONS OF PARTNERSHIP

The reasons for promoting collaboration between home and school are the same in the case of parents of children with special needs as they are in the case of other parents: they have the right to be involved in their children's schooling; and their children receive better education when they are involved. These considerations are, if anything, stronger when the children have special needs. If young people have limited powers of comprehension or self-advocacy, parents are likely to have a greater role in securing their interests and to need to exercise that role for a longer period than would otherwise be the case. Because of their special needs, teaching them requires careful planning and detailed monitoring of progress. In the case of some pupils, such as those with emotional/behavioural problems or severe learning difficulties, there is considerable overlap between the concerns of home and school. All this points to the need for a dovetailing of their respective approaches. This will lead to a consistency of treatment between home and school and will ensure that the different adults impinging on a child's life work in harmony and reinforce each other's efforts.

What form should the collaboration take? It is clear from what has been said so far that many kinds of collaboration or partnership are possible. As an aside, it is worth noting that the concept of equal partners, as espoused in the Warnock Report, is not particularly helpful here. As a general term indicating equality of regard between home and school, it does have a place, but it can smack of empty rhetoric and be misleading in practice. The Warnock chapter on 'Parents and partners' does in fact paint an asymmetrical picture of the partnership. Parents of children with special needs are seen to require three main forms of support – information, advice and practical help. Whilst this support should be given in a co-operative way with account being taken of the contribution that parents can make, the prevailing emphasis is one of teachers and other professionals helping parents to cope better.

Five dimensions of partnership are being proposed here, focussed, respectively, on:

1. Information.
2. The curriculum.
3. Behaviour problems.
4. Personal support.
5. Liaison with professionals.

With the exception of personal support, it is possible to envisage an equality of partnership in each of these and to regard it as an ideal to inform good practice. Such equality is not always necessary however, and in some cases will be neither feasible nor helpful in practice.

Information

A first step in partnership, which provides the essential basis for collaborative working, is the sharing of information. Parents of children with special educational needs should have received a good deal of information before they come into contact with the school. They should have been given an understanding of the nature of their child's difficulties and the educational implications of any impairments they may have. They should have been made aware of local facilities and, in particular, the educational provision available for pupils with special needs. They should know which schools have particular expertise and where to go for specific details.

Schools may well have to supply much of this information, but they have also to provide a great deal of further information on the work of the school and the progress of pupils within it. A good deal of information can usefully be given in written form – indeed the 1980 Act requires schools to publish sufficient information to enable parents to make informed decisions about them. Often the information given on special needs provision is sketchy, particularly in comparison with public examination results (if good).

Likewise when schools hold open days, the tendency is to highlight the facilities for the most able pupils. This is understandable in the context of schools competing in the market-place of declining pupil members, but it does make it harder for parents to find the information they need if their child has difficulties in learning.

Whatever written information is available, it should be supplemented by oral presentations and, above all, by dialogue where parents can relate the official information to their own situation. The formal language of curriculum statements may convey very little to parents, whereas an informal question-and-answer session can give them a good idea of what is going on in class. Good access to teachers is vital here, where ready opportunities exist for parents to ask whatever is on their mind.

The flow of information does not have to be one-way. Teachers benefit from knowing about the home background and being aware of relevant factors in it that affect a child's response to schooling. When pupils live in difficult home situations it is imperative that teachers have a proper understanding of this. Teachers can use their contact with the home in assessing the success or otherwise of teaching programmes.

Good, two-way information has many spin-offs. Apart from laying the foundation for more sustained collaboration, it promotes the sense of a shared enterprise. It is particularly helpful for parents to know that there is mutual understanding and exchange of information and that the information they themselves have to offer is taken seriously. It also helps in anticipating problems and resolving them when they do arise.

The curriculum

There are many programmes designed to secure the active involvement of parents in delivering the curriculum and to ensure that the work of the school is carried on in the home. These range from highly structured activities such as Portage to *ad hoc* and informal contact. Portage is a home teaching programme that involves parents and professionals in a carefully planned partnership. It covers a wide range of early development and lends itself to working systematically through agreed aspects of development. Other formal programmes are often focussed on language, with parents reinforcing and supplementing school work in the natural language situations arising at home. If pupils are using a signing system to communicate at school, they benefit from the opportunity to practise using it at home. Topping and Wolfendale (1985) describe a large number of initiatives on parental involvement in pupils' reading.

A school's input to home can also be relatively unstructured. Some schools make use of home-school books to propose specific activities for carrying out at home and to build on the work done in school. They can be the basis of regular daily or weekly homework or they can be a means of reinforcing particular pieces of work on an occasional basis. They can also be used to ask parents about particular activities in the home or obtain feedback on specific programmes. Many schools appreciate the importance of enlisting the support of parents and ensuring that they back up the work of school – providing good models for speech, stimulating the child appropriately, reinforcing independence programmes, and not colluding in immature behaviour.

Parental involvement in the curriculum can also take the form of input by parents to the work of school. Parents can contribute to curriculum planning by developing, in discussion with teachers, a more detailed understanding of their children's strengths and weaknesses, what teaching approaches are likely to be effective with them, and how they are actually responding to various approaches. This contribution can be made in a more formal way if parents are given a say in curriculum design or sit on curriculum planning groups, though this is not yet common practice.

Parents can play a significant role in the delivery of the curriculum in schools. At a basic level, they can supply resources either directly or through fundraising activities. This is often the only form of parental input to the curriculum, and many schools and parents are more than content that it should be so. There are examples, however, of parents providing major support in the classroom – hearing children read, carrying out ancillary tasks, and even co-teaching. This type of involvement raises difficult questions about parental competence and the availability of training, the separation between home and school in the child's perception, the usurping of waged jobs by voluntary workers and the local authority's commitment to providing adequate staffing levels. It is without question that parents can give considerable direct support to class teaching, but there are problems and costs that must be taken into account.

Finally, parents can play a major role in the school's monitoring of children's progress. They can provide information on a child's behaviour and activities at home, which is important in evaluating the school's effort with the child and establishing how well he or she is putting into general practice what is being taught at school. This information can be conveyed by means of home–school books or through occasional chats with the teacher. Formal review meetings offer a forum where this can be done in a public and detailed way. Many schools now hold such review meetings on a regular basis where everybody dealing with the child makes an input. When parents are enabled to participate in these meetings, not only can they hear the professionals' reports at first hand, and if necessary question them, but can place their own observations, suggestions and practices before the group.

Behaviour problems

Dealing with behaviour problems can be viewed as a particular aspect of partnership over the curriculum. It is especially important for pupils who have emotional and behavioural difficulties, but can arise also in the case of pupils whose learning is attended with difficulty and frustration or whose impairments are such as to impede normal social learning. Integration introduces major responsibilities in this regard. If a pupil is being educated in an integrated setting as opposed to a residential school, programmes designed to control and modify behaviour can only be implemented for part of the school day. In some cases this is insufficient, and it may be necessary to involve the family explicitly in management programmes.

Teachers differ in their attitudes to this. Some are reluctant to involve themselves in the home situation. There is a risk of intruding in the relationship between parent and child by introducing systematic teaching or behaviour management programmes. It is common, too, for children to have separate standards of behaviour at home and school, and reports of untoward behaviour at home may seem to have little relevance in school. There is a common view that, whilst helping parents manage their children is a legitimate task for the school, it has to be a secondary concern. Crises and instances of untoward behaviour may necessitate intervention, but in the normal run of events such teachers place their major emphasis on the cognitive domain.

A radically different approach is taken by others who regard the distinction between the cognitive and affective domains as having little relevance for many pupils. These teachers attach high priority to working with parents in order to learn from them and to assist them in managing any behaviour problems. This may entail detailed work with parents, including, possibly, observation and dialogue in the home, to identify the precise nature of pupils' behaviour problems and work out ways of dealing with them. For younger children the Portage home teaching programme referred to above lends itself well to being used in this context. Some teachers invite parents to the classroom so that they can observe how the teacher deals with behaviour problems; this is not necessarily to tell the parents how they should do it, but rather to illustrate basic principles of behaviour management and give them a fresh perspective on coping with their child's behaviour at home.

The passage of information and advice should not be one-way, not least because of the fact that some behaviour problems are exacerbated if not caused by the school. Insensitive handling and inappropriate discipline can lead to negative situations that might have been avoided. There should be no doubt that schools create emotional and behavioural difficulties in pupils, just as they create learning difficulties. If there are good channels of communication between parents and school this is far more likely to happen, and when difficulties do arise frank discussion between parents and teachers may provide concrete suggestions for dealing with them and ensuring that they do not develop into major problems.

Personal support

Bringing up a child with special needs can be difficult, and some parents need support as individuals in their own right. This is different from the support – through giving information and advice – that enables parents to play an effective role in their child's education. It is rather to acknowledge the range of demands made on them – as one parent put it, 'our highs are higher and our lows are lower'. This does not mean treating them, any more than their pupils, as totally special cases. There are times, however, when some parents benefit, both in their role as parents and as collaborators in their child's education, from a degree of extra support and understanding. This can come from the professionals involved with their children, who for the most part are teachers, and from other parents.

Teachers can play an important role in assisting parents to view their child realistically and accept his or her limitations. They are possibly in a unique position to do this since parents relate more easily to them than to other professionals – and also they (teachers) are more likely to discuss the child in terms that the parents can understand. Because of their experience teachers are well-placed to help parents take a long-term perspective. Parents of course have a long-term awareness of their own children that no one else can have, but the very intensity of this does sometimes mean that they are overcome by present difficulties. This is where the teacher who is concerned and informed but not emotionally involved can assist with a necessary balance and detachment. In some situations the teacher's role is simply to be a sympathetic listener. Teachers must be careful here since they are not usually trained to provide counselling or social work support – and in any case they seldom have the time to do it properly. There will be occasions, however, when simple humanity requires that teachers provide a shoulder to lean on because nobody else with the necessary detachment is available.

Support of a different kind is provided by contact with other parents of children with special needs. Their common experiences enable them to understand and support each other in mutually helpful ways. This can take the form of straightforward social contact, simply giving parents the sense of belonging to a group, or it can be an opportunity for sharing experiences and providing mutual reassurance and encouragement. Some schools make special efforts to facilitate contact between parents through coffee mornings, open days, and the like. Integration can help in this respect since, whilst the total number of parents with children with special needs may be less than in a special school, they are likely to have readier access to the school. It also tends to lead to the informal contact that is so valued by many parents.

Liaison with professional agencies

Many pupils with special needs are involved with Health and Social Services as well as Education, and a given family can have dealings with a large number of agencies. This presents problems for both parents and school. For parents it can mean relating to a large number of professionals, an experience many find confusing if not intimidating. As far as the school is concerned, it becomes only one of many agencies dealing with the pupil and not necessarily the most authoritative one.

Teachers have a significant go-between role here and can provide a valuable link between parents and professionals. They can help parents to find their way round the system, explain their rights to them, and interpret official information and reports. They can also assist in practical ways such as facilitating appointments, helping with transport and securing allowances.

How important an element of partnership is this role? Many of the functions it entails fall outside the teacher role as normally conceived. Teachers may feel that they have neither the time nor the expertise to carry them out properly. The key question is whether they should be carrying them out or not. Certainly, teachers could fulfil this role if they were timetabled for it and given the necessary training. A critical consideration must be what happens when parents are given no support in their dealings with professional agencies. On past experience, many will continue to play a marginal role in their child's schooling and will not gain full benefit from the services available to them. In addition, none of the other dimensions of partnership outlined is likely to develop to any significant degree.

The Warnock Report did in fact envisage such a role. It proposed that all parents of children with special needs should be able to look to a 'Named Person' who would 'provide them with a single point of contact with the local education service and expert counsel in following their child's progress through school' (9.27). It was recommended that for most children the Named Person should be the head teacher of their current school or another staff member who was versed in special needs education. It was hoped that this recommendation would be incorporated into the Education Act 1981 but, despite considerable lobbying by parent groups, it was in the end excluded. Whether or not this work is recognised and resourced, it still needs to be done. If nobody else is concerned to do it, it falls – as with much else – to the lot of individual teachers to do it as best they can.

ATTITUDES OF PARENTS

So much for what parental partnership entails. But do parents actually want it? Do they aspire to be partners in their children's schooling and take on roles hitherto seen as the preserve of the school?

It would be easy to make out a negative case here. A great many parents regard schooling as the business of teachers and express no desire to be involved in it. If pressed they would doubtless say that they do not possess the necessary skills. It would, however, be needlessly defeatist to accept such a negative case without question. There is a growing body of evidence that parents value the opportunity to be involved when it is presented appropriately. They may need guidance and encouragement to begin with, but the chances are that if they are given a meaningful role they will seize it and will come to place a high value on their contact with school.

Wolfendale (1987) has reviewed some of the evidence on the attitudes of parents who *had* been involved in various programmes. The general picture is one of enthusiastic endorsement. Both parents of children with special needs and other parents were positive about their experiences and believed that they, as well as their pupils, had benefited. The principal feature distinguishing these parents was simply that they were given the opportunity for involvement, and it seems reasonable to suppose that a great many of the people who are currently non-committal or negative about parental involvement would also appreciate the benefits if given the chance. Widlake (1986) refers to the suspicion barrier between home and school, and quotes numerous examples where it proved to be groundless and where straightforward initiatives elicited strongly supportive attitudes from parents.

Consideration of attitudes to parental involvement raises the question of attitudes to integration. This is of primary concern to the relatively small number of parents for whose children special school and ordinary school are real alternatives. It does raise wider issues however. The debate on the relative merits and demerits of special schools and ordinary schools is in many ways a political one, and parental attitudes and wishes have become an important element in the argument. For this reason too parental attitudes are an important determinant of the rate at which the necessary reforms will be carried out.

Aside from the polemics and the institutional considerations, there are also individual concerns. These are primarily issues to do with parents' perceptions of their own child and how these might be affected by type of school placement. When a child is born its parents' lives are changed forever. If the child is not 'normal' the changes are ones they will not have anticipated and will not welcome. Some feel their lives are blighted and face years of painful readjustment to expectation. Many parents do make a successful adjustment and come to recognise and cherish their child's individuality. This task is often made more difficult by the very support agencies that should facilitate it. When major institutions such as schooling remove children from the local community and insist on providing for them apart from the mainstream, the effect is to underline the extent to which they are special and different.

Integration can help in this regard. It enables children with special needs to attend the local neighbourhood school, alongside peers and be part of the local community. This does not remove their special needs but it places them in perspective. Parents are well aware of the need for specialist attention, but the way in which it is given can make a big difference. If it is in a context of normality where the child engages in some activities alongside peers, parents benefit from knowing that occasionally at least their child is just 'one of the others'. The handicapped identity ascribed by society is not constantly being reinforced, and parents are helped to see their child as an individual who happens to have special needs.

But isn't all of this rather idealistic? What about those ordinary schools where the child who is different stands out like a sore thumb and has the fact that he or she is different marked out at every turn? By placing pupils with special needs in an ordinary school are we not ensuring that their singularity is emphasised, whereas if they went to a special school they would be undistinguished alongside children with comparable special needs? Is it not the case also that many parents *want* special schooling and consciously choose it for their child (as indeed is their right under the Education Act 1981)? Are there not some parents who are disenchanted with ordinary schools and regret having sent their child to one?

Certainly there are ordinary schools that are grossly unsuited to pupils with special needs, and parents who have horror stories to tell. Equally there are very good ordinary schools and parents who could not be more pleased with the education their child has received. Anecdote and counter-anecdote pile up here, generating more heat than light. But how is the matter to be resolved? This is not an academic debating point that can be shelved once aired. The education of real children is at stake, and decisions are constantly being taken that enhance or diminish the quality of the education they receive.

First of all, the arguments about the existence of 'bad schools' need to be addressed – and dismissed. It cannot be doubted that there are bad schools, and it would be callous to ignore the negative educational experiences that some children have in them. These are irrelevant to the argument however – despite their frequent citing by those who would oppose integration – just as the existence of bad doctors does not negate the value of medicine. (If there were many such schools or if the general experience of children with special needs in ordinary schools was negative, one could question the timeliness of integration though not necessarily the principle.) No one wants any child to go to a bad school or to have a negative experience of schooling, and parents who reject this for their children with special needs are not necessarily opposed to integration. In seeking an alternative form of schooling they may well be exercising a positive option that many parents of children in the catchment area of such a school would like to have.

At a more general level, the appropriate response to poor schools has to be to improve them. An individual parent may well decide to abandon a school, but that is seldom an option for the responsible authority. If schools are failing particular pupils with special needs, the likelihood is that they are failing many other pupils as well. What is required then is not a retreat behind the barriers of special schooling but a reform of ordinary schooling.

Secondly, the evidence on parents' preferences in respect of integration has to be examined. Here too anecdotes abound – and must be discounted if a balanced view is to be obtained. There are particular problems of measurement. Apart from the general difficulties associated with measuring attitudes, parents often have experience of either special schools or ordinary schools but not both – or if their child has been to both, their experience of them is asymmetrical – so their attitudes toward the two sectors will not be impartial. Preference is conditioned by knowledge of and familiarity with what is available. It is to be expected that parents of children in special schools will tend to favour special schools and assume that the requisite expertise can only be found there. Thus, a majority of special school parents (21 out of a sample of 35) in Sandow and Stafford's (1986) study rejected the idea of integration. Similarly, ordinary school parents are likely to be disposed in favour of ordinary schools.

So a straightfoward cataloguing of attitudes for and against is not especially helpful and does not resolve the issue. What *does* matter is the attitudes of parents with substantial experience of ordinary school placements for their children. If there is a presumption in favour of integration – with alternatives having to justify themselves – the key question is how parents of children in ordinary schools regard ordinary schools. If their attitudes are positive and well-founded, it is somewhat academic whether their attitudes are stronger or weaker than the attitudes of special school parents toward special schools.

A study conducted at NFER threw up some striking information here (Hegarty and Pocklington, 1981). A total of 43 sets of parents were interviewed in their homes, and *every single one* wanted their child to continue his or her education in an ordinary school. The children varied greatly in their special needs – physical and sensory impairment, communication disorder, moderate and severe learning difficulties – and in their experience of schooling. Some had just started school while others were about to leave, having experienced a range of educational settings, including special schools, along the way. Some were individually integrated into a mainstream class, others were attached to a unit or special class in an ordinary school, and still others were integrating from a special school base. In other words, they were a cross-section of pupils with marked special needs attending ordinary schools and, whilst the sample was small, the unanimity of parents' views was remarkable.

The theme of normality kept cropping up with these parents. It may not be very easy to spell out what is normal but they clearly wanted their child to do ordinary things as much as possible and 'have a part in life with other children'. Just going along to school with other children from the neighbourhood was valued for its own sake. They pointed to some specific advantages. Many commented on how their child had come out of a shell and generally grown up as a result of mixing with ordinary children. An aspect of maturing particularly valued by parents was the greater independence that they felt integration promoted. This was a central concern as children grew older and parents had thought to the future. It is salutary to note the generally robust attitude parents had to teasing: not only were they unconcerned about it but some even ventured that they were going to have to become used to ignorant people in later life and they might as well start at school.

Some parents with a wider concern for society's acceptance of people who are different argued that the presence of pupils with special needs in ordinary schools was a critical step in changing societal attitudes. It demonstrated that they could cope with normal institutions and gave the lie to many myths of helplessness. It was also highly functional since it enabled 'normal' children to have regular, unfussy contact with those who were different and be rid of the fears and misconceptions that bedevil many adults' attitudes.

There was a strong concern for academic progress as well, with parents anxious that their child should receive as good an education as possible. The vast majority in fact were delighted with their child's progress. Parents commented particularly on improvements in speech and language. One of the most striking pointers to emerge came from those few parents who were not satisfied with their child's academic progress. In spite of their dissatisfactions, and in spite of having poor opinions of particular teachers, they remained committed to integration and *still* wanted their child to go to an ordinary school (not necessarily the one they were now attending!).

The policies of parent associations provide another significant indicator of parental attitude. There are a good many of these associations, mostly organised around particular types of special need. Traditionally, they have tended not to favour integration. Their concern has been to get services established for their children, sometimes even to have their right to education acknowledged. In many respects they have been highly successful in achieving this aim. The result, however, is a considerable personal and material investment in segregated institutions, including special schools. These are often of high quality, sometimes indeed pioneering new forms of service delivery. It is all the more notable then that parent associations are beginning to take integration seriously, formally adopting policies of integration and looking actively at how they might redirect their resources and their campaigning.

The International League of Societies for Persons with Mental Handicap (ILSMH) is a good case in point. This is an umbrella organisation for national and other societies concerned with mental handicap. In 1983 it set up an Integrated Education Sub-Committee to assemble information on practice relating to integration in different countries and to make recommendations. A position paper has been produced that affirms the right of children with severe learning difficulties to integrated education. The development of integrated educational services is seen as an important step toward normalisation. Even when local conditions make this development difficult, integrated education must remain the target to aim for and every effort should be made to move toward it.

PROMOTING PARTNERSHIP

Given the growing importance attached to home–school partnership and the wide range of functions it can serve, ways have to be found of building it up. Mittler and Mittler (1982) make a number of practical suggestions for promoting partnership. These are based on examples of current practice and are geared to the different facets of schooling. In a further paper Mittler (1987) offers a set of questions relating to each of the following seven facets:

1. Parents' priorities.
2. Access to school staff.
3. School meetings.
4. Home visiting.
5. Home–school diaries.
6. School reports.
7. Parent workshops.

The list is too extensive to reproduce in full but a few sample questions will give the flavour:

How often are parents invited into the classroom
– to observe their child?
– to share in the teaching of their child?
– to take part in classroom activities?
What proportion of parents have attended school meetings in the past term?
How many parents were visited at home last term?
What information is included in home–school diaries?
– behaviour? activities? physical achievement? suggestions for joint activities?

These suggestions and questions offer a very useful starting point for any school that wants to develop this area of work. They are not prescriptive but are intended rather to facilitate the task of reviewing policies and practices in relation to developing partnership with parents. Where practice is thin or non-existent they point the way ahead and reduce the development task to discrete, manageable proportions. Where practice is already well developed they provide a framework for critical self-analysis.

Seligman (1979) offers detailed guidance to teachers on working with parents of pupils with special needs. This is based on practice in the United States but has considerable relevance to this country as well. He argues that the role of the teacher must extend beyond teaching, if only because of the impact of legislation. (Since 1975 parents in the United States must be a member of the team that approves the child's educational programme and decides on placement. As a result contact between parents and school has become far more frequent.) The book is concerned to equip teachers with the requisite skills and presents a great deal of practical material directed toward that end. There is a particular focus on interviewing skills with material on establishing rapport, attending to non-verbal behaviour, encouraging people to talk, asking questions and so on. Examples and critical incidents are presented to stimulate discussion and role playing.

In conclusion, some general principles emerging from the NFER study cited above (Hegarty and Pocklington, 1981) may be noted. First, parents must be put at ease. Too often professionals forget how daunting they and their expertise appear to parents. Teachers must remember that school is perceived as alien territory by many parents, and as a result they are ill at ease and find it difficult to be their natural selves. For some it will bring back memories of their own unsuccessful school-days and of teachers who believed in keeping parents at a distance. A first priority then is to take the steps necessary to remove any social barriers that parents may experience and ensure that they are in a position to interact with teachers and other professionals in a positive and natural way.

Secondly, all concerned – teachers and parents – must believe in collaboration! This may seem an obvious requirement but it is worth affirming none the less. A great deal of lip-service has been paid to the idea of parents as partners, and special efforts may be necessary to reassure parents that their involvement is genuinely sought. Teachers must recognise that parents have a unique contribution to make and where necessary convince parents that this is so. Many parents have a view of education as a highly skilled process in which they have no part. It is conducted in schools by expert teachers with occasional inputs from even more skilled professionals. For this reason it may be necessary to engage in a bit of demystifying, explaining to parents that, whilst their child may have special needs and stands to benefit from specialist intervention, much can be done that does not require specialist intervention and indeed there is a great deal that is better done by parents.

Having encouraged and motivated parents, the next step is to establish the tasks to be carried out. There are various criteria for appropriate tasks. It goes without saying that they should fall within the parents' competence to execute them, with instruction and explanation as necessary. It is unhelpful – and may well be dangerous – if parents are engaged in work that has not been properly explained to them. There is, in any case, little point in setting up tasks that parents do not understand. The tasks must be meaningful to parents and have a clear relevance to the child's needs. If they cannot see the rationale for what they are doing, it will be difficult for them to maintain motivation and carry out the tasks effectively. The work assigned must also be consonant with the fact that it is being done by parents and must not interfere unduly with the parental role. Children with special needs also need parents! It would be most unfortunate if parents were to become so intensively involved in these tasks that pupils had teachers at school *and* teachers at home.

Whatever tasks are worked out, teachers must take them seriously and give the necessary input of time and effort to back them up. They must be introduced to parents and explained to them in terms they understand. The tasks can be set in a variety of ways – home–school books; home visits; formal sessions in school, possibly including other parents as well – which should be selected to fit the individual situation. The objectives in mind, the resources available and the particular circumstances of the family must all be taken into account. When a task is straightforward and is well understood by parents, regular entries in a home–school book may suffice. If the task requires significant input from parents, possibly needing to be incorporated into the family's routine in ways that require thoughtful planning, then occasional home visits may be helpful.

Finally, teachers must maintain their commitment to the activity, partly to encourage parents and partly to monitor what is going on. It is tempting for teachers to wash their hands of a programme when it is up and running, especially as they are often not timetabled for this involvement. It is important that they resist the temptation however. Parents need continual reassurance that what they are doing is important and useful. They are likely to want to discuss the programme from time to time and make sure that they are doing the right things. As the professional responsible, the teacher has a duty to monitor progress and intervene as necessary.

Costs and resources

MONEY MAKES THE WORLD GO ROUND!

Education costs money. Where pupils with special needs are concerned it can cost a great deal. Specialist staff dealing with very small groups or even individuals, new or modified buildings, additional curriculum material, equipment ranging from cassette recorders to adapted microcomputers, special transport arrangements – all of this can add up to very considerable levels of expenditure. This impinges directly on the integration debate because new demands are being made on schools and local authorities at a time when resources are under pressure, and also because integration is sometimes seen as primarily a means of reducing or at least containing expenditure on special education.

Some may argue that children's needs are paramount and that questions of cost should not be allowed to determine how they are met. Once a given package of resources has been judged necessary for a pupil, the effort must be to ensure that the package is supplied regardless of expense. In an ideal world, where resources were limitless, this would be fine. In any case, considerations of cost should not be allowed to drive out educational considerations in deciding on levels of provision since that would disadvantage those whose needs are greatest.

We do not live in an ideal world however. It is idle to think that the education of pupils with special needs can be decided entirely on educational grounds to the exclusion of financial ones. Educational resources are limited in supply, and those required for pupils with special needs can be quite scarce. This may reflect an 'absolute' scarcity – such as in skill areas like speech therapy where there are too few trained personnel – or it may signify a society's unwillingness to provide resources beyond a certain level. Whichever is the case, nothing is gained from adopting an ostrich-like attitude and ignoring the exigencies of financial constraints. If a particular resource, such as speech therapy, is simply not available, alternative ways of using the resources to hand must be explored in order to meet pupils' needs in some other way. If the problem is one of political will, the task is to argue for more resources. In either case, resources and how they are used are central to the business of education. It behoves educators to be aware of this and to know how resources are allocated in practice. There are many competing demands on public spending, and educators must make their voices heard if they want to influence the patterns of resource allocation.

Another perspective here comes from viewing integration simply as an alternative way of allocating resources and developing the implications for practice that flow from that. Special schooling entails a concentration of resources that, under integrated arrangements, are necessarily dispersed. This is not a neutral question in terms of educational provision, since the way in which resources are made available affects how they can be used and may impinge on their effectiveness. Thus a physiotherapist in a special school will work in a different way from one who pays periodic visits to individual pupils in a large number of ordinary schools; it is likely that the nature of the service offered by this resource and its relationship to the rest of the curriculum will be quite different in the two cases. Numerous similar examples could be adduced where the pattern of resourcing, costs and the nature of the provision are inextricably linked.

This chapter, then, is about costs and resources. It outlines an accounting framework for examining the cost of different forms of special needs provision. The purpose of this is not to give instruction on drawing up balance sheets but to assist in identifying the cost-incurring elements of provision. It can be extremely difficult to identify the exact cost of a form of provision, and any figures arrived at are likely to need careful interpretation. What educators need is to be able to analyse a provision in terms of its resources and be conversant with the resource implications of making specific changes. This puts them in a stronger position both to monitor the use of existing resources and to make the case for additional resources. In this context, the often-asked question: Which is cheaper – integration or segregation? becomes far less important. It emerges indeed that this question is neither helpful nor particularly important. Finally, the chapter looks at a number of dilemmas thrown up by the funding of special needs provision.

AN ACCOUNTING FRAMEWORK

The first task is to establish a framework for looking at costs. This entails a detailed description of provision in terms of elements that incur cost or the utilisation of resources. (Some significant inputs may not lend themselves to quantification in cost terms.) These elements must then be set within an appropriate structure. Hegarty and Pocklington (1981) proposed a grouping under four broad headings: (i) staff and professional services; (ii) premises; (iii) resources and equipment; and (iv) transport. These were elaborated in some detail and include elements such as the following:

Staff

This is the main source of expenditure, covering teaching, care and other staff, both full-time and part-time.

- salaries and wages
- training expenses
- other staff-related costs including travelling

Premises

This includes teaching and non-teaching accommodation, the latter covering everything from mobility and care arrangements to swimming pools.

- new purpose-built accommodation
- major adaptations to existing buildings
- minor alterations, such as constructing ramps, adapting toilets, modifying doorways
- furniture and fittings
- operational costs such as fuel, maintenance, loan charges

Resources and equipment

Some requirements will be the same as for other pupils but depending on individuals' special needs many additional items may be required.

- books and other printed materials, including tests
- educational equipment, including cassette recorders and micro-computers
- adapted equipment as required for physical education, craft subjects, domestic science, science, and music
- handicap-specific items, including wheelchairs and other mobility aids, typewriters adapted as required, low vision aids, hearing aids

Transport

This is important in integration but frequently a problem and an obstacle to full participation in the life of the school.

- journeys to and from school, possibly including escorts
- travel during the school day, on split sites or when schools are linked
- trips and extra-curricular activities.

WHAT DOES IT ACTUALLY COST?

Given an agreed framework for examining costs, it might seem a relatively straightforward matter to assign actual values and state how much a particular form of provision costs. There are considerable difficulties however, both analytical and practical. Firstly, it is necessary to be clear about the provision being costed and what exactly it comprises. Particularly when a provision encompasses pupils who would have been at the school anyway, there is a degree of arbitrariness in what is included for costing purposes and what is excluded. Secondly, there are practical difficulties to do with obtaining the requisite figures in a meaningful form.

Defining the exact nature of the special provision is central to the costing exercise since this determines how costs are to be apportioned between it and the rest of the school. This is relatively easy if the provision is self-contained within the school. So long as pupils in a special class or unit do not make use of mainstream facilities and so long as their teachers and ancillary staff provide no services to other pupils, the cost of the provision can be established by apportioning overhead costs on a pro-rata basis, possibly adjusted to take account of the fact that pupils with special needs make greater use of overhead facilities, and adding on to the direct costs of providing for these pupils. In most cases, however, no such simplicity is possible. Even when the provision in question is 'integration' in the sense of catering for pupils who would otherwise have attended a special school, it is not usually cut off from the rest of the school in a way that would enable it to be treated as a separate cost centre. There is a two-way movement of pupils and staff across its boundaries, and often a sharing of resources and expertise as well. It would, in principle, be possible to disentangle the costs by keeping a sufficiently detailed record of all transactions across the boundary, though this would hardly be feasible in practice.

A more intractable situation presents itself when the provision for special needs has become an integral part of the school, catering for all pupils with learning difficulties of whatever kind within the school. Some pupils – the traditional clientele of special needs provision – may receive substantial attention, but with others there is only occasional or short-term involvement. The latter, who can be a sizeable group (20 per cent or more of the student body), are often pupils who would not receive this level of specialist input if the special needs provision had not been established at the school. A further feature is that all staff are staff *of the school* and divide their time flexibly between pupils with special needs and others. In addition, some special needs support is likely to be given by staff not formally assigned to special needs work.

Defining the special needs provision for costing purposes is problematic under these circumstances. The more the provision becomes an integral part of the school, the less feasible it is to separate it from the rest of the school's work. Pushing to the limit, how does one distinguish between carefully planned teaching geared to the individual needs of each pupil and special provision conceived as something additional? The upshot of all this is that it can be extremely difficult to isolate the costs attributable to special needs provision with any accuracy, and that in certain respects it may be inappropriate to do so anyway.

As for obtaining actual figures, there are a number of practical difficulties. First, the figures have to be assembled from a number of sources. Schools rarely have the requisite information nor do they often have access to it. Special needs provision may be receiving a variety of inputs from Education – school psychological service, advisory support team, education welfare officers, transport – plus medical and paramedical services from Health and social work input from Social Services. Information has to be extracted from all of these sources in order to give a full picture.

A second problem is that many of those responsible for the different inputs do not have the figures either, any more than the schools, or they do not have them ready to hand. It is hard enough to obtain figures relating to an entire school; obtaining them for *part* of a school may be difficult in the extreme. This is likely to be particularly so in the case of Health and Social Services inputs which will themselves generally be part-time.

A third difficulty is that the figures that are available may well be unsuitable. Information on school costs, for instance, is geared to treasurers' concerns and local authority financial planning rather than to the running of individual schools. More generally, there is no common basis for the financial information being assembled from the different sources. This is a problem even within Education since there is no agreed formula for school costing. Health and Social Services involvement bring in yet further accounting procedures. The net result of all of this is that a great deal of work may still be necessary after the figures have been obtained. They have to be re-calculated onto a common basis in order to convert them into a useable form.

USING FINANCIAL INFORMATION

The enumeration of difficulties may lead to the conclusion that the whole enterprise is simply not worth while – and justify the traditional educator's stance of regarding costs as a closed book. That would be an unfortunate outcome. Whilst it is sometimes necessary to grapple with the difficulties and produce a detailed costing, what is often required is something quite different.

Teachers need a comprehensive view of the services they provide if they are to be effective advocates for them. Particularly if services are under pressure or if expansion is being sought, they must have a good understanding of the resource context. They must be able to relate resources to desired outcomes and indicate the likely impact of specific changes. An accounting framework such as presented here helps teachers in these tasks by identifying the cost-incurring elements of programmes and giving a structure for relating costs to the other constituent elements.

Costs and resources must not be seen in isolation. The analysis of educational costs only makes sense in the light of a broader analysis of the provision being costed. There are no set formulae for deciding what a particular form of provision should cost or how much should be spent on different categories of pupils. There are some rules of thumb, based on the size of the teaching group (and therefore pupil–teacher ratio) conventionally deemed appropriate for different types of special needs – hearing impairment, communication disorder, and so on. (The fact that the pupil–teacher ratio varies so much even within a given special needs grouping is a potent illustration of the arbitrary nature of these rules.) These are no more than rules of thumb however. They do not provide bench-marks either for establishing or for evaluating levels of provision. The costs attributed to a given provision only make sense in the light of the local situation, and any useful interpretation of them must be based on a detailed analysis of that actual provision.

There are a few general principles to guide interpretation. Firstly, the state of development of the provision must be taken into account. Costs are generally greater at the beginning, at least on a per capita basis. Pupil numbers build up gradually as admission criteria and procedures are developed and the pattern of provision is worked out in detail. Staff are engaged in training, developing the curriculum, acquiring resources and building up liaison with colleagues, and there is less time for pupil contact. Consequently, staff productivity as it were is lower and the cost per pupil higher than it will be later. Furthermore, there may be considerable non-recurrent expenditure at the outset on building alterations, equipment, and major resource items.

Secondly, some costs are quite specific to a given provision and may not be relevant elsewhere. Transport is a fairly obvious example. In dispersed rural areas, taking children to school can represent a considerable expense. Staff costs likewise may be affected since, if lengthy periods are spent travelling, peripatetic services will need higher staffing levels for the same number of pupils. A catchment area may have characteristics that add to the demands made on special needs provision. Take a language unit serving a socioeconomically depressed area. If a majority of the children (and their families) require social work support is this a legitimate charge on the language unit? It may be that this support is an important part of the whole programme and would not be available if the unit did not exist, but equally it might not be necessary if the unit were in a more favoured area. Accommodation is another aspect of provision where costs may be highly idiosyncratic. If spare space of a suitable kind is available, savings can be effected by using it; in other localities extensive alterations or even purpose-built accommodation may be necessary in order to make the same level of provision.

In addition to these specifics of time and place, there is a further consideration related to the *net* cost of educating pupils with special needs. This can be analysed at several levels. At its most basic, these pupils would have to be educated anyway, regardless of whether they were deemed to have special needs or not; the costs represented by this have to be offset against the gross costs to get a measure of how much extra their education requires. Precisely how this is done and what difference it makes depend on the alternatives deemed to be available. The most clear-cut situation is where the alternative is placement in an independent school where the local authority is paying a determinate – and sizeable – fee. (Given the level of fees, especially for residential schools, the net effect of developing integrated provision is sometimes to save the authority money.) For many pupils, the alternative is placement in one of the authority's own special schools. For others, the most likely alternative is attendance at an ordinary school with no particular account being taken of their learning difficulties.

A final consideration relates to the costs incurred in system change. These are illustrated by the situation in special schools, which is affected by developments in ordinary schools. Special schools have had to develop a range of new functions, as we have seen in chapter 9, and establish new ways of working with different client groups. Some have to be maintained with reduced numbers. Others have to close. Each of these situations has particular implications for both the overhead and the direct costs of pupils' education, and it is necessary to take account of them in calculating unit costs.

At a more general level, implementing changes in patterns of provision takes time, and there can be a considerable period of overlap when services are duplicated. This inevitably pushes up unit costs for a time. It is important to distinguish between costs that derive from system change and those directly attributable to educating pupils. Innovation may be inhibited if this is not done: maintenance costs are not separated out from start-up costs, with the result that the innovation may be judged to be more expensive than it actually is.

COST COMPARISONS

Does integration save money, or does it cost more in the long run? Is it a cheaper, more cost-effective way of educating pupils with special needs? Or does special schooling offer economies of scale that are lost when pupils are dispersed into ordinary schools?

These questions only concern a relatively small number of pupils with special needs, but they have to be addressed because of the widespread interest in comparing segregated and integrated provision. We saw in chapter 5 that there have been numerous comparative studies focussed on different aspects of academic achievement and social development. Cost comparisons focus on the perfectly understandable desire to maximise the use of resources. This is seldom a neutral, technical exercise: many parents and teachers are suspicious about official enthusiasm for integration, sometimes claiming that it conceals an intention of cutting expenditure and providing special education on the cheap. Whatever the political dimension of cost comparisons, it should be realised that both parents and teachers face major technical and other difficulties.

Firstly, there are the technical problems associated with establishing the costs of provision, as outlined above. To carry out a comparison, all the costs attributable to educating comparable groups of pupils in segregated and integrated settings respectively must be identified and related to each other. This is a formidable accounting exercise: it has to encompass staffing and professional services, premises and capital costs, material resources and transport; it must cover a reasonable time span that will fairly represent typical costs in both cases; particularly in the case of integrated settings, it has to isolate the costs attributable to the groups from global costs; and it should take due account of the marginal costs in both cases.

If we assume that the accounting problems can be solved, there are still major difficulties of interpretation. These boil down to the near impossibility of ensuring that we are comparing like with like. Great efforts have gone into improving provision for pupils with special needs in recent years. As a result integration programmes are often implemented in a context of improved provision, or one where special education is being extended to pupils who would not previously – or otherwise – have received it. Furthermore, the way in which the service is delivered can vary enormously between integrated and segregated settings. Take, for instance, a department for pupils with moderate learning difficulties in a comprehensive school as compared with the secondary department of an ESN(M) school. Whilst both may have the same formal remit, viz. to educate secondary-age pupils with moderate learning difficulties, it is likely that there will be so many differences in curricular provision, mode of working, other duties carried out by staff, and so on, that any direct comparison of costs will be meaningless.

A further difficulty is that some important variables are not quantifiable, in monetary terms at least. These relate to both inputs and outputs. It might, for instance, be easier to involve parents in their children's education in integrated settings, simply because there is likely to be easier access to them. On the other hand, it could well be argued that the concentration of specialist staff and pupils with the wide range of special needs found in a special school is essential to maintaining the supply of skilled teachers. Yet neither of these inputs could be located easily in an accounting framework. The same holds true for many of the outcomes of education, particularly those relating to social and emotional development.

FUNDING DILEMMAS – SPECIAL PLEADING OR SHARED HARDSHIP?

The funding of special needs provision poses a number of dilemmas. Like other activities paid for out of the public purse, it is underfunded and the aspirations of many in the service are constrained by cash limits. In this respect, it is no different from housing, health services, social services, or mainstream education.

There are particular considerations, however, arising out of the relationship to mainstream provision. These revolve around the problem of providing pupils with the extra resources they need without singling them out unduly. By definition – pupils are deemed to have special educational needs if additional provision is required for them – their education entails higher than average levels of support. The danger in practice is that providing this support singles them out in negative ways and isolates them from peers. This can happen with any aspect of provision but is especially pointed where resourcing is concerned. (The fight for improved provision is often synonymous with the fight for more resources.) This can be examined in relation to three areas of costing: (i) earmarking funds for specific purposes; (ii) raising funds from private sources; and (iii) paying special allowances to teachers.

Funds for special needs provision in ordinary schools have typically been earmarked, i.e. treated as additional to the school's main funds and kept quite separate from them. Historically this is perfectly reasonable. Special needs provision is commonly introduced to a school as an extra, catering for pupils who would not otherwise attend that school. Sometimes, though this is becoming less common, the staff concerned do not even report to the head teacher but to an adviser, education officer, or other person outside the school. Its successful establishment, moreover, depends on funds being available from some source different from the mainstream school budget. This is usually a special education budget that is administered quite separately from primary and secondary school budgets.

There are several advantages to such separate funding – over and above the fact that it enables new provision to be set up! Firstly, it makes it clear to the school that the special needs provision will not be a drain on its resources, and may even strengthen them by bringing along items that can be used in common. This is important since many people believe that the education of other pupils will suffer when special needs provision is introduced to a school, and anything that demonstrates that their fears are groundless is to be welcomed. Secondly, earmarking funds gives greater control over spending and helps to ensure that the monies are spent as planned. If the resources allocated for pupils with special needs are absorbed into the overall school budget, there is no guarantee that pupils with special needs will continue to benefit or receive the extra support intended for them. This is particularly likely to happen in a large school where, ironically, the absorption of special needs funding would make little difference to the school. Expenditure on special needs provision has generally been spared in the recent cuts in educational spending, and the fear is that this might no longer hold true. The protection afforded by earmarking would disappear, and the allocation of funds would depend on individual, local priorities.

A further consideration sometimes put forward is that patterns of expenditure as between special needs provision and the main school are very different. It is, therefore, administratively simpler to keep them separate. Certainly there are differences. Thus, special needs provision may be receiving inputs from outside Education and will often be using staff more flexibly than the main school. It is a moot point, however, whether these differences make sufficient impact on the *running* of the school to merit separate financing arrangments.

There are a number of objections to the earmarking of funds, some on practical grounds and one on a fundamental issue of principle. On the practical side, few special needs provisions are totally cut off and there is generally some sharing of resources. Maintaining a strict separation is often not feasible – and becomes less so as the sharing increases. Take a teacher who divides teaching time between the special needs provision and the mainstream on a flexible basis, or classrooms that are used by different groups at different times of the day. In such cases, the allocation of costs between special and mainstream becomes highly problematic and a little arbitrary – the more so as the special needs provision becomes an integral part of the school. Moreover, separate funding can lead to wasteful duplication or the under-utilisation of expensive items such as television sets and microcomputers and also of curriculum materials.

The fundamental objection to earmarking is that it reinforces and exaggerates the separateness of special needs provision. Apart from the practical barriers set up by separate funding arrangements, they carry a symbolic message as well: special needs provision *is* separate from the main school, and any links or overlap are between independent entities. This perception keeps pupils with special needs at arm's length and hinders the progress of integration. If a provision for special needs is to be fully part of the school and pupils with special needs are to take their place alongside peers, this must be reflected in the financial and administrative arrangements as in other ways. If the goal is a single school making differentiated provision for varying needs, then materials and resources must be acquired and held in common by the school as a whole.

Similar considerations apply to fundraising. Whilst public education is free and paid for from public sources, many schools seek additional funds from parents and other voluntary sources to supplement their grant from the local education authority. This gives them some freedom to experiment and enables them to provide a wide range of educational 'extras' – school trips, library books, microcomputers, and so on. (Increasingly, schools are complaining that as cuts in educational expenditure go deeper this supplementary income, intended to enhance the school's educational provision, is being diverted to making good deficiencies in basic provision.) Special schools benefit particularly in this regard since they constitute a 'good cause' and capitalise on the public's charitable impulses. Many special schools rely on money raised through fundraising activities or from charitable donations to finance building improvements and major items such as minibuses. Some head teachers of special schools see it as an essential part of their job to raise money in this way. In doing so, they do not, of course, play down their pupils' deficiencies; if anything they highlight them. Wheelchairs and sightless eyes make for more effective fund-raising than stressing what the pupils can do and how much they have in common with other pupils.

A very different situation obtains when these pupils attend ordinary schools. Their learning difficulties are no less than before and they are just as likely to benefit from the extras that cannot be provided by means of capitation or other public funds. What is the head teacher or teacher in charge to do? Should they seek to capitalise on the fundraising potential of pupils with special needs – thereby singling them out and running the risk of isolating them? Or should they accept that part of the price of having them in an ordinary school is that less resources will be available for their education? The first course of action goes counter to the principle of integration and would call into question the point of placing the pupils in an ordinary school in the first place, whereas the second works against the best interests of individual pupils.

In practice, the dilemma is seldom as black and white as this, but there can be considerable tension none the less as schools strive to provide high quality education in as near normal environments as possible. This tension is, if anything, accentuated by the increasing dependence of schools on funds from parents' associations and the like. If pupils with special needs consume a disproportionate amount of any extra funding, should they not help to generate it in the same measure? It could be argued that educational authorities should take account of the likely reduction in voluntary funding when pupils with special needs are absorbed into the mainstream and pay a corresponding supplement. Given the prevailing ambivalence – extending well beyond education – toward voluntary contributions and the confusion over the dividing line between public and private sector activity, this is unlikely to happen. It is, however, the logical response of effective commitment to integrating pupils with special needs into ordinary schools.

Special allowances to teachers represent a minor cost, but not one to be dismissed lightly! In fact, they pose exactly the same dilemma as earmarking and fundraising, and do so in a very pointed way. All teachers working in special schools are still paid an extra allowance. (Because of the smaller size of the special schools there are also relatively more opportunities for promotion to senior posts.) Teachers responsible for special needs in ordinary schools may or may not be receiving such an allowance – it depends entirely on local practice. This is hardly satisfactory in a profession where conditions of service are negotiated nationally, and leads to teachers feeling aggrieved when neighbouring colleagues doing similar work receive an allowance that they do not.

Is there a case to be made for paying special allowances to teachers in ordinary schools? Those in favour point to the difficulty and demands of the job and the need for special training in order to do it effectively. Then there is the matter of parity: the special school allowance has established the precedent of extra payment for teaching certain kinds of pupils, and their teachers expect this payment to be made regardless of whether they are in special schools or ordinary schools. Recruitment could be affected, since suitably experienced staff might be reluctant to move from special schools if they lose their allowance in the process. In any case, some special needs provisions have been set up by means of a formal transfer of pupils and staff from a special school, and teachers have naturally continued to receive their allowances.

The case against allowances is considerable however. Why should teachers in the special needs area be singled out for such favourable treatment? The alleged difficulty of the work is hardly a sufficient reason. Other teachers too face difficult tasks, often with inferior working conditions. (And what if it were demonstrated that teachers in the special needs area had easier workloads?!) As for specialisms, teachers of mathematics, science, music, and so on are specialists just as much – and frequently have more specialist training in their subject area than special needs staff have in theirs.

The fundamental objection, however, is that the payment of allowances is divisive and contrary to the spirit of integration. The integration of pupils is hardly fostered by the segregation of staff. If the special needs teachers are really part of the school they should be subject to the same conditions of service as everybody else. What is to happen when pupils with special needs are taught by mainstream staff? Do the latter qualify for a share of the special allowance?! It is easy to see that the payment of allowances to staff at ordinary schools leads to anomalies and even absurdities.

As to parity between teachers in special schools and ordinary schools, the only way to resolve this is to grasp the nettle of allowances and abolish them for all teachers. This would remove a major divisive factor at a stroke. It is unlikely to affect recruitment to the special school sector, though it would make it easier for staff to consider a transfer from a special school to an ordinary school. It would be unpopular with special schools of course but it need not be all loss. An alternative arrangement might be proposed that would fit better with the standard conditions of service: teachers could receive extra payment in respect of recognised qualifications in special education. This would be to link any extra rewards to competence in doing the job rather than to the location in which the job was done – a procedure whose fairness could hardly be called into question.

The Future

Looking ahead

Predicting the future is an uncertain business, and is probably best left to those who need votes or cheap headlines. We cannot escape its backward shadow, however. Social reform is impelled as much by the vision of a better future as it is by a jaundiced view of the present. It is salutary, too, to examine present trends and see where they are likely to lead us – if nuclear winter or socioeconomic collapse do not intervene. The most likely future scenario may not be to our liking, and that knowledge may help us to avert it.

This chapter therefore introduces some speculations on special needs provision – what future is there for special schools? how should schools prepare pupils with special needs for adult life? how will the new information technologies affect schooling? It begins with a caveat on the danger of over-campaigning for special needs provision, and ends by emphasising the importance of a committed teacher workforce if the desired reform of schools is to be achieved.

SPECIAL NEEDS IN CONTEXT

Special needs provision is only one of many challenges facing schools. Examination reform, multicultural education, parental and community involvement, technical and vocational education, equal opportunities for girls, new information technologies, drugs education, teacher appraisal – the list goes on and on. Schools are at the receiving end of a growing number of central government initiatives. They are subject to a succession of reorganisations consequent on demographic shifts, political dictates, and changing patterns of post-16 provision. They are under increasing pressure from politicians, the general public, and pundits of all sorts to become more relevant, to solve society's ills and generally to prepare young people for working and living in a post-industrial society.

Where does special needs provision fit in here? The remarkable thing, perhaps, is that it is on the agenda at all, and that it occupies so central a position on it. Schools have many pressing concerns, and it is no small achievement that provision for pupils with special needs ranks high amongst them.

There are dangers to avoid. Special needs provision has been neglected and under-resourced in ordinary schools for many years. Not only did schools fail to make appropriate provision for pupils with special needs but they attached low priority to doing so. Now that the special needs star is in the ascendant, the temptation is to brook no restrictions in making up for the years of neglect.

This is problematic on two counts. First, it could be counter-productive: resource demands that are perceived to be unrealistic can build up resistance to meeting even reasonable demands. Secondly, there are difficulties of principle. The resources available to education are finite and, whilst advocacy to increase the proportion allocated to a particular sector is proper and even necessary, the effort to secure more must follow certain ground rules. This means arguing the case on *educational* and not humanitarian or other grounds. Advocates for special needs provision must realise that they are not the only ones with legitimate demands for more resources, just as people with impairments have to learn that they are not the only ones with problems in life. If they do not, the result will be special pleading – and ultimately back to segregation. Extra provision becomes a gift based on charitable impulses rather than an entitlement based on identified educational needs.

There is a further consideration still that must temper campaigning for special needs provision. Campaigning may be necessary at the moment because of past inadequacies, but the object must be to make itself redundant. The goal in view has to be one where special needs provision disappears from the vocabulary of schooling. This may seem Utopian, if not perverse in a book that has sought to argue the case for building up such provision. As long as pupils who have difficulties in learning are regarded as special cases, however, neither they nor the provision made for them will be fully part of the school.

Pupils with special needs are so designated because they need provision over and above what the school normally provides. The 1981 Act is carefully neutral in referring to provision that is 'additional to, or otherwise different from' the school's normal provision. Too often, however, special needs provision attracts a negative connotation, and reformers must take care that they do not unwittingly reinforce the very thing they are trying to eliminate.

Children are different from each other, and the effective school is providing for each according to need *as part of its normal provision.* Certain provision will be required by some pupils only, but whether this be remedial tuition in reading or advanced instruction on the violin it must be seen as an integral part of the school. If special needs provision is treated in this way, it will become invisible within a school at the same time as it is serving pupils' needs most appropriately.

SPECIAL SCHOOLS

What is going to become of special schools? We have seen in chapter 9 how they can help ordinary schools in providing for pupils with special needs. This is not a sufficient role, however. The argument developed in this book would suggest a limited future for them: as ordinary school reform builds up the competence to educate pupils with more complex educational needs, special schools will become redundant.

This is where theoretical argument must face up to practical reality. There can be no doubt but that special schools will be part of the map of special needs provision for the foreseeable future. The number of special schools has dropped in recent years and will fall further. Much of this is attributable to the fall in school rolls, and the widespread closures once feared by many special school teachers have not materialised. It is likely that the new legislation and the various pressures for integration outlined above will lead to a substantial reduction in the number of special schools. This will happen gradually, however, and we shall not see a sudden switch in resources that, in countries like Italy, has led to the rapid closure of large numbers of special schools.

Whatever the number of special schools in the future, we can safely assume that they will be different from today's special schools. Some of the changes will be highly visible, such as the greater use of technology, especially computer-based technology, which will move beyond aids to communication and mobility and become fully integrated into the learning process. School buildings will be of a higher standard as elderly and unsuitable premises are taken out of service. A consequence of the smaller number of special schools will be an increase in the amount of travel to and from school and possibly in the number of pupils having to stay in residential accommodation.

The client group will also be different. As more pupils with special needs attend ordinary school, the ones remaining in special schools will be those with the greatest and most complex learning difficulties. This will push up unit costs since there will be need of more individual attention and probably more expensive material resources as well. It will necessitate better trained and more expert staff since these pupils pose the greatest teaching challenge.

More significantly, it will force major changes in the nature of the special school. In particular, it will invalidate the established way in which schools are grouped by handicapping condition – hearing impairment, physical handicap, moderate learning difficulties and so on. Such disability-grouped schools have always had some pupils on roll with more than one handicapping condition. Schools for the visually impaired, for instance, often have on roll a few pupils who are hearing impaired as well and deal with them as best they can.

The future scenario is one where there will be far more such pupils. It may well be that special schools will have a majority of pupils whose learning difficulties stem from several different sources (in terms of the traditional categories). We have already seen in chapter 2 that the link between handicapping condition and special educational need can anyway be indirect and tenuous. That fact called into question the traditional way of organising provision for pupils with special needs. What we have here is a further reason for modifying the traditional way. If this nettle is grasped – and it will be a radical undertaking – special schools in the future could be organised quite differently. They could, for instance, operate on an area basis, catering for pupils with a wide range of learning needs in a given area, or they could attempt to work to a new mapping of special educational need based on pupils' requirement of specialist teaching.

Further structural changes are likely to come from the new functions that special schools are taking on. Chapter 9 outlined the range of new functions in respect of supporting the ordinary school and the structural changes that follow from this. These developments will continue, and if anything intensify. A related development is the emergence of the special school as a resource centre. This can be for curriculum development, inservice training, the collection and evaluation of equipment and computer software, specialist assessment, and advice and consultation on all matters relating to the education of pupils with special needs. These resource centre functions are important in improving the standard of special education provision regardless of where it is provided. They make it possible to capitalise on experience and establish a bank of information, resources and expertise. They are particularly relevant for ordinary schools who have only a few pupils with marked special needs on roll and do not have ready opportunity to build up the necessary knowledge and expertise themselves.

All of these developments point to a new kind of institution, quite different in kind from the conventional school be it special or ordinary. This must comprise elements of the teachers' centre, the advisory service and the pilot project, but it has other strands as well that do not have institutional analogues in the world of education. This suggests metamorphosis rather than evolution, and the emergence of a support structure that is quite different from the existing special school and does not follow naturally from it. The institutional shape that the structure, or structures, will take depends on which of the various functions outlined above will be given priority and cannot safely be predicted at the moment. What is clear is that these institutions must be highly resourced and staffed by skilled professionals. If they are to become a credible force in provision for special needs they must both innovate and base themselves on the best of current practice.

BECOMING AN ADULT

Unemployment is a major fact of contemporary life. The scarcity of jobs hits school leavers particularly hard. In some localities it is only the exceptions that find paid work when they leave school. Youngsters who have had difficulty in learning are at a particular disadvantage. Not only are the numbers of unskilled and semi-skilled jobs declining but there is more competition for those that are available. School leavers who have had learning difficulties are likely to be up against relatively more able peers who would previously have been going for skilled jobs. Because of the general presumption in favour of qualifications, their limited academic attainments are likely to count against them even for manual work with little academic content.

How is the school to respond to this situation? Clearly, it cannot shut its eyes and carry on as before in the hope that full employment will return. It won't. Short of a highly unlikely social and technological revolution, structural long-term unemployment is here to stay. May and Hughes (1985) paint a grim picture of the prospect facing young people with moderate learning difficulties. The best they can expect is

> a series of short lived placements on various government sponsored schemes of dubious meaning and value, punctuated by successive and growing periods of unemployment as they move further beyond the range of the emergency measures set up to assist the post-school transition.
>
> (page 158)

Schools face two sharply contrasting options here – make the curriculum more vocational so that young people are better equipped for the available jobs, or reduce the vocational element in favour of preparation for a lifestyle where paid work is less important than it is today. Both approaches have their advocates – and each arouses fierce opposition. The first is castigated for its functional view of education and its irrelevance, the second for its woolly thinking and its defeatist mediocrity.

The vocational approach is widely favoured in current practice, as school leavers' courses increasingly base themselves on vocationalism. This applies to all school leavers, not just those with special needs, as demonstrated by the rapid growth of the Technical and Vocational Education Initiative. By giving young people work experience and equipping them with skills for the workplace, it is hoped that they will have the edge when competing for scarce jobs. In its most sophisticated form this entails *transferable* skills so that the young people can cope with a variety of jobs and also adapt flexibly within particular jobs as the requirements of the workplace change.

The trouble with this approach is that it ducks the central reality of too few jobs. It may do at the micro level, and may be all that is possible for the individual school. But it will not do as a general strategy. If all schools prepare young people effectively for the labour market, and no jobs are available, nothing will have changed – except that the unemployed will be better qualified (for work, not necessarily for unemployment).

The opposite approach is to prepare young people for unemployment, not just in the passive sense of alerting them to its likelihood but of consciously building up the attitudes, knowledge and skills that fit them for a life not shaped by paid work. What exactly should this preparation comprise? The Warnock Report saw the 'secret of significant living without work' in helping other people – the lonely, the vulnerable and the handicapped (10.127). Admirable though such altruism might be, it sets a standard by which few of us live our entire lives. Massie (1982) emphasises the importance of having control over one's life, though he does not spell out the implications for education.

Dyson (1985) would base the curriculum on the traditional notion of a liberal education, something of intrinsic worth to be pursued in its own right. His concern is with the quality of life and with education as the means by which it is transformed. The focus is on what people are rather than what they can do, on the process of learning rather than its outcomes. He recalls Peters' (1973) dictum: 'To be educated is not to have arrived at a destination; it is to travel with a different view'. This concept of education is, moreover, as relevant to pupils with special needs as to anybody else.

The challenge is to weave these strands into a coherent and motivating educational programme. It means helping young people to discover all their capacities and start on the lifelong task of developing them. It means freeing them from domination by their immediate surroundings and unlocking new worlds of experience, feeling, and insight. It means replacing work preparation with preparation for the constructive use of time, community involvement, and personal relationships.

There must be a corresponding set of changes in the so-called hidden curriculum, since this is where attitudes and values are formed to a significant degree. There is a deep-seated assumption in schools – as in society at large – that paid work is good and necessary; by implication its absence is bad and associated with failure. As long as schools continue to base themselves on this assumption, it will be impossible for young people to free themselves from the expectations it sets – and that society does not permit them to achieve. Schools must not only educate young people in a broader way: they must be committed to education as the most relevant form of preparation for adult life that they can give. Otherwise, the hidden curriculum and what is taught in lessons will be out of step with each other, and young people will end up with the worst of both worlds.

Such a reform of the curriculum will not be achieved easily, not least because many oppose it. Some reject it as Utopian and claim that, even if it is desirable, it cannot be achieved. Others question its desirability. They can point to the fact that there will always be some jobs and some young people who will get them. The latter will presumably need to be orientated to the world of work while still at school. This is likely to create two classes of pupil – those who will have jobs and those who won't – and could be as damagingly divisive as any of the handicap categories.

More fundamentally, this curriculum reform cannot be achieved without a corresponding reconstruction of societal values and patterns of distribution of wealth. At the moment, having a job is an important part of adult life – it confers income and the independence that goes with it, it is a major occasion for social contact, and it gives a sense of self-worth and of social legitimacy in the eyes of others. Unless society finds alternative ways of conferring adult status on young people, schools that give little attention to the world of work risk being dangerously out of touch. Whilst the hegemonic power of the work ethic is startling in some respects, given the constricting boredom of so much work, there is little evidence of the popular support necessary to reshape values and attitudes nor of the political will to restructure access to material goods.

Does this mean that the reforming school is destined to swim fruitlessly against the tide? To accept that would be to concur in the current bankruptcy of public policy in respect of youth unemployment. Schools may not be very powerful as agents of social change but they do have a contribution to make. At the lowest level, they can stop reinforcing the centrality of paid employment. They should make sure that they do not foster false expectations and prepare young people for roles they will never fulfil. But there is a more positive challenge. Schools can promote new concepts of socially useful work and upgrade the status of co-operation and participation in the community. They can help young people to realise their creative potential and equip them for active leisure.

None of this will make much difference unless the economic infrastructure is sorted out. But change must start somewhere. And school is as good a place as any if the target is a society where productivity is measured in terms of human and not just material output.

NEW INFORMATION TECHNOLOGIES

No look to the future would be complete without some speculation on technological developments. This is partly because of their near-magical qualities – we marvel that the blind see and the deaf hear – and partly because, whatever their underlying complexity, the outcomes are plainly visible and easy to understand. This distinguishes them from broader sociocultural changes that may be far more significant in the long run but which emerge gradually and over a wide canvas, and are therefore less evident or comprehensible.

If such speculation is to be useful it must take account of sociocultural and economic realities. It must concern itself with what is practically possible rather than with what is technically feasible. Most technological functions that a layman might dream up for a futuristic scenario are probably already technically possible – but not affordable or robust enough for everyday use. The trick is to predict which technological developments will move outside the laboratory or the specific military application and – even more difficult – how they will be used.

One safe prediction is that technological aids in general will be more widely available in the future. This depends crucially of course, as do all predictions of this nature, on the stability of the world political and economic order. If we assume that the relative peace and prosperity enjoyed by the developed countries will continue, the year 2000 will see far more developments and greater access to them in the fields of telecommunications, office automation, entertainment, and domestic life. For people with special needs, there are three areas of prime concern, viz. communication, mobility, and daily living arrangements. We can anticipate advances in hearing aid technology, computerised brailling, personal transport, and control over the environment, especially the domestic environment. All of these will add to the quality of life and enable more people to lead full and independent lives.

What about young people and their experience of schooling? How will this be affected by the new technology? What are the implications for educating pupils with special needs in the ordinary school?

Again it is relatively safe to predict that school children of the future will live in a more sophisticated technological environment, both at home and at school. The gap between home and school, exemplified by the greater access to microcomputers and video recorders in the former, will probably increase if present trends continue. This could lead to significant problems of mismatch in children's perceptions and cognitive styles. It is not necessary to indulge in McLuhanesque rhetoric to envisage conflict between an early upbringing and home life dominated by images and values from the media and a school ethos shaped around the written word and traditional academic values.

Developments in technology and increased access to them will be of particular benefit to pupils with special needs and will make it easier for them to attend ordinary schools. Advances in the twin factors of mobility and environmental control will eliminate or minimise many of the problems of physical access to and within buildings, particularly as older premises are taken out of service. These gains, which affect primarily those who are blind or physically disabled, are easiest to achieve in new purpose-built buildings that can incorporate, for instance, sensors for echo location guides, remote control devices for opening and shutting doors, and non-intrusive automated stair lifts.

Advances in communication technology will make it easier for pupils who are blind or deaf to attend ordinary schools, both as regards teaching and learning in the mainstream classroom and as regards interacting with peers. Visual display units attached to voice-sensitive aids could revolutionise communication for those who are deaf or physically disabled and help to breach the wall of silence that so often isolates them in mainstream settings. Those who are blind can expect similar benefits from optical character recognition devices whereby written text is translated into other forms, possibly including intelligible speech. Aids to communication offer a spin-off bonus in that they facilitate note-taking, personal record keeping, and drafting written work. Difficulties in these areas often inhibit pupils' independent study and learning, and these advances will play a significant role in permitting effective participation in mainstream learning.

The primary business of schooling is the teaching and learning that go on in the classroom. Developments that bear directly on classroom activities will, in the long run, be the most significant, albeit less dramatic than some of the advances in mobility and environmental control. They are also more diffuse and therefore harder to predict. There is a wide, and growing, range of computer software available to schools, some of it subject specific, some geared to general developmental stages. The challenge is to ensure that this new resource goes beyond gimmickry and does really facilitate pupil learning.

There are two main problems with current classroom applications of microcomputers. First, much of the available software is, for all its quantity, educationally inadequate. There is little to be gained from using a microcomputer to do in a cumbersome fashion something that can be done perfectly well by other means. Many 'educational' programs are based on traditional ways of packaging knowledge and learning, and fail to exploit the potential of the microcomputer. Secondly, computer assisted learning is frequently not related to theories of learning and classroom practice. These are not separate problems. The reason so much educational software is valueless is that programs have been devised without reference to relevant theory – in child development, pedagogy, and so on – and without taking account of how they will be used in practice. If these problems are resolved, computer applications in the classroom will be very different in the future. There will be an abundance of *relevant* software, that will be educationally valuable and will offer pupils unique ways of interacting with learning material.

Two developments in particular will facilitate this happening, one technical, one related to the dissemination of information. Developments in programming languages will enable teachers to write their own software or make significant inputs to the process and also to 'customise' standard software for their own purposes. As serious classroom use of computers grows and practice-related evaluation becomes established (the Centre for the Evaluation of Information Technology in Education at NFER is a good example of how the two activities fit together), there will be a dynamic body of proven software and good practice to disseminate. Electronic mail and related networks will help ensure that this information is widely distributed and easily accessed by practitioners.

All this has particular relevance to educating pupils with special needs in the ordinary school. Their prime need is for appropriate individual attention that can be provided relatively economically and without unduly singling them out from peers. Computers can assist in this process in a great many ways. Possible examples

range from drill-and-practice programs to sophisticated computer simulations.

Take first the learning of basic skills that so preoccupies teachers
of pupils with learning difficulties. Many of these pupils need vast
amounts of practice in basic skills, often to an extent that the adults
involved find extremely tedious. Using teachers to provide it is in
fact neither necessary nor effective, even if they have time and the
patience to do it. Any skill that can be broken down into
component parts is, in principle, programmable so that different
pupils are given individual practice schedules. Not only can these
be geared precisely to individuals' stages of learning and endlessly
varied to avoid pupil boredom, but they can also incorporate
continual – and tireless! – monitoring and adaptation to keep in step
with individuals' progress.

Precision teaching based on behaviour modification principles
lends itself in a major way to being supported by microcomputers. It
entails teaching to a carefully specified set of objectives where
teaching and monitoring are closely and frequently related to the
objectives. Programmes of work are drawn up which are based on
detailed task analysis and geared specifically to individual pupil
needs. Appropriate computer software can help both in carrying
out the task analyses and in matching up the steps to individual
pupils' learning situations. Computers can help with task analysis
in two ways: directly, by modelling the behaviour to be analysed
and displaying the elements of behaviour for different levels of
analysis; and indirectly, by storing and retrieving the results of
previous analyses. If the behaviour to be learnt is broken down into
fine steps, computers offer a powerful way of monitoring pupils'
progress along the steps and ensuring that what they are asked to
do is at each stage carefully matched to what they are ready to do.

If pupils with special needs are to be taught alongside peers in
mainstream settings, they must have comparable access to the
curriculum. This can be particularly problematic in the case of those
who have sensory or physical impairments. It is precisely the
difficulty of providing adequate access that has so often been used
to justify segregated education. The capacity of microcomputers to
generate and control simulations can also help here in offering an
alternative to missing sense modalities and compensating for
experiences that pupils cannot have.

A more general point relates to the role of specialists and the
extent to which they can be replaced by technology. The scarcity of
some specialist expertise is a major factor inhibiting good practice in
integration. One function of computers, however, is to 'capture'
skill: by routinising a sequence of activities into a computer
program, a skill can be detached from the skilled person and made

more widely available. There are already startling applications where the work of skilled craftsmen has been captured in this way and is now performed by machines run by supervisors who do not have the skills in questions.

Human beings are not production line artefacts, and tentative experiments in psychiatric counselling and medical diagnosis show how much more difficult such skill capture becomes when dealing with people. It would be naive to suppose that advances will not be made however. Many activities of psychologists, speech therapists, physiotherapists, and specialist teachers of all sorts lend themselves to routinisation, and one can envisage a future scenario where powerful computer software will provide schools with instant access to a great deal of expertise that is now available only intermittently. After all, if speech therapists and physiotherapists can 'program' an untrained classroom assistant to do some of their work for them, it is reasonable to suppose that intelligent computers of the future will also be able to carry out some of their functions.

WILL THE REVOLUTION HAPPEN?

Reform has been the burden of this book. Primary and secondary schools have been failing to meet the needs of many pupils, and may indeed have been adding to them. Neither legislation not rhetoric will, on their own, do much to stop this. If schools are to make adequate provision for pupils with special needs, radical changes are called for – in the curriculum and academic organisation of schools, in the allocation of resources, in teacher training, in the structure and functioning of local authority support services, and so on.

Are these reforms going to happen? Is the goal of one school for all, with full back-up services, really achievable? Is it sensible to expect that changes on the scale envisaged can be brought about at a time when schools are facing so many other pressures?

The answer is simple at one level. The revolution has already started. Examples can be found in practice of any given aspect of the desired reform. Schools and authorities exist to show that well-re-sourced schools catering adequately for a wide range of special educational needs can be established. So the questions for the future, whatever they may be, are not questions of feasibility. They have to do rather with translating into practical action what we know to be possible.

The critical element in all of this is the professional quality of the teaching force. More than any other single factor, this will determine whether the reform will gather momentum and lead to a unified but richly varied educational system providing flexibly for all pupils within the framework of a common school and a common curriculum, or whether it will peter out and leave existing good practice as isolated pockets of excellence. There is more at stake here than the training and professional development of teachers as discussed in chapter 10. Current initiatives, though modest, certainly enhance teachers' knowledge and skills and they do have the potential to make a major contribution to the professionalism of the teaching force. Competence is not enough however. There is also the question of morale and commitment, which are essential elements of dynamic professional performance in any sphere of work.

It is hard to doubt the general consensus that morale in the teaching force in Britain is at its lowest level for many years, and it would be foolish to assume that the road back up will be easy. The prolonged industrial action of 1985/86 and teachers' perceptions of their low status in the national labour market that have both fed and been reinforced by it will cast a long shadow. No matter what settlement is reached, the aftermath will see a different spirit in schools. The mere ending of the dispute will not in itself restore teacher morale. Indeed, the effort to spell out contractual duties could well lead to many teachers doing the required minimum and no more.

Special needs provision in the narrow sense has been protected from much of the industrial action. This is small consolation, however, if the goal is to achieve whole-school reform. Pupils with special needs are the concern of all staff, and work with them must be subject to the same conditions of employment as any other work in the school. If the future lies in spelling out contractual duties, provision for special needs must be written in as an integral part of these duties.

The stakes are high. It is not a question of persuading teachers to give more consideration to a small group of pupils who have hitherto been marginal, important though that is. It is much more to do with giving teaching its proper regard as one of the most worthwhile and challenging human activities, instrumental in securing the stability and prosperity of the nation but – more importantly – of intrinsic value in its own right.

Neither teachers nor politicians nor the general public appear to believe this at the moment, and therein lies the greatest threat facing the education system. Teaching must be rehabilitated. Unless the practice, and the profession, of teaching are valued, education will continue to suffer – and everything in our national life that is held to depend on good education will be at risk. It is ironic that provision for special needs may be the means whereby this happens. The growing realisation that pupils who have difficulty in learning require superior teaching skills and the impact of such skills on schools affirm the signal importance of good teaching. This provides a framework for the renewal of schools in which better provision for pupils with special needs is part of enhancing the education offered to all pupils.

References

Adams, F. (ed.) (1986) *Special Education*. Harlow: Longman.

Advisory Committee on the Supply and Education of Teachers (ACSET) (1984) *Teacher Training and Special Educational Needs*. London: Department of Education and Science.

Better Schools. See Great Britain, House of Commons (1985).

Blythman, M. (1985) 'National initiatives: the Scottish experience' in J. Sayer and N. Jones (eds) *Teacher Training and Special Educational Needs*. London: Croom Helm.

Bolam, R., Smith, G. and Canter, H. (1978) *Local Education Authority Advisers and the Mechanisms of Innovation*. Windsor: NFER.

Booth, T. (1982) *Special Biographies*. Milton Keynes: Open University Press.

Chapman, E. (1982) A new approach to the training of teachers with special needs. *Educational Review* (34) **2**, pp. 161–168.

Clunies-Ross, L. and Wimhurst, S. (1983) *The Right Balance: Provision for Slow Learners in Secondary Schools*. Windsor: NFER-Nelson.

Colbourne Brown, M. and Tobin, M. (1983) Integration of the educationally blind: parents' rights and general conclusions. *The New Beacon*, July, **LXVII**, pp. 169–174.

Colby, M. and Gulliver, J. (1985) 'Whose remedies, whose ills?' in C. Smith (1985).

Croll, P. and Moses, D. (1985) *One in Five: The Assessment and Incidence of Special Educational Needs*. London: Routledge & Kegan Paul.

Davies, J. (1980) Physiotherapy in ordinary schools. *Special Education: Forward Trends* (7)**1**, pp. 29–31.

Department of Education and Science (DES) (1967) *Children and Their Primary Schools* (Plowden Report). London: HMSO.

Department of Education and Science (DES) (1968) *Psychologists in Education Services* (Summerfield Report). London: HMSO.

Department of Education and Science (DES) (1972) *The Education of the Visually Handicapped* (Vernon Report). London: HMSO.

Department of Education and Science (DES) (1977) *A New Partnership for Our Schools* (Taylor Report). London: HMSO.

Department of Education and Science (DES) (1978) *Special Educational Needs* (Warnock Report). London: HMSO.

Department of Education and Science (DES) (1983) *The In-service Teacher Training Grants Scheme* (Circular 3/83). London: DES.

Department of Education and Science (DES) (1984a) *Initial Teacher Training: Approved Courses* (Circular 3/84). London: DES.

Department of Education and Science (DES) (1984b) *The In-service Teacher Training Grants Scheme* (Circular 4/84). London: DES.

Department of Education and Science (DES) (1985a) *The Curriculum from 5 to 16: Curriculum Matters 2*. London: HMSO.

Department of Education and Science (DES) (1985b) *The In-service Teacher Training Grants Scheme* (Circular 3/85). London: DES.
Department of Education and Science (DES) (1986a) *The Local Education Authority Training Grants Scheme: Financial Year 1987/88* (Circular 6/86). London: DES.
Department of Education and Science (DES) (1986b) *Lower Attaining Pupils Programme (LAPP): Issues for Discussion*. London: DES.
Department of Education and Science (DES) and Department of Health and Social Security (DHSS) (1983) *Assessments and Statements of Special Needs* (Circular 1/83). London: DES.
Dust, K. and Moses, D. (1986) In-service education for specialist teachers of children with special educational needs: a survey of the diploma courses 1984–85. *Research Papers in Education* (1) **3**, pp. 194–216.
Dyson, A. (1985) A curriculum for the 'educated man'? *British Journal of Special Education* (12) **4**, pp. 138–139.
Enderby, P. and Philipp, R. (1986) Speech and language handicap: towards knowing the size of the problem. *British Journal of Disorders of Communication* (v) **21**, pp. 151–165.
Gipps, C., Gross, H. and Goldstein, H. (1987) *Warnock's 18%: Children with Special Needs in Primary Schools*. Brighton: Falmer Press.
Great Britain, House of Commons (1985) *Better Schools*. London: HMSO.
Gulliford, R. (1986) The training of teachers in special education. *European Journal of Special Needs Education* (1) **2**.
Hallmark, N. and Dessent, T. (1982) A special education service centre. *Special Education: Forward Trends* (9) **1**, pp. 6–8.
Hargreaves, D. (1982) *The Challenge for the Comprehensive School*. London: Routledge & Kegan Paul.
Hegarty, S. and Lucas, D. (1978) *Able to Learn? The Pursuit of Culture-fair Assessment*. Windsor: NFER.
Hegarty, S. and Moses, D. (eds) (1988) *Developing Expertise: INSET for Special Needs*. Windsor: NFER-Nelson.
Hegarty, S. and Pocklington, K. with Lucas, D. (1981) *Educating Pupils with Special Needs in the Ordinary School*. Windsor: NFER-Nelson.
Hegarty, S. and Pocklington, K. with Lucas, D. (1982) *Integration in Action*. Windsor: NFER-Nelson.
HMI (1986) *Report on the Survey of the Lower Attaining Pupils Programme: The First Two Years*. London: DES.
Hodgson, A., Clunies-Ross, L. and Hegarty, S. (1984) *Learning Together: Teaching Pupils with Special Educational Needs in the Ordinary Schools*. Windsor: NFER-Nelson.
Inner London Education Authority (ILEA) (1984) *Improving Secondary Schools*. London: ILEA.
Inner London Education Authority (ILEA) (1985) *Educational Opportunities for All?* London: ILEA.
Jamieson, M., Parlett, M. and Pocklington, K. (1977) *Towards Integration: A Study of Blind and Partially Sighted Children in Ordinary Schools*. Windsor: NFER.
Jowett, S., Hegarty, S. and Moses, D. (1988) *Joining Forces: A Study of Links Between Special and Ordinary Schools*. Windsor: NFER-Nelson.
Kramer, J. (1985) The 1981 Education Act in Derbyshire. *British Journal of Special Education* (12) **3**, pp. 98–101.

Kramer, J. (1987) Special educational needs and the voluntary groups. *European Journal of Special Needs Education* **2** (1).

Laskier, M. (1985) 'The changing role of the remedial teacher' in C. Smith (ed.) *New Directions in Remedial Education*. Brighton: Falmer Press.

Massie, B. (1982) Significant living without Warnock. *Special Education: Forward Trends* (9) **3**, pp. 27–29.

May, D. and Hughes, D. (1985) The prospects on leaving school for the mildly mentally handicapped. *British Journal of Special Education* (12) **4**, pp. 151–158.

Mercer, J. and Lewis, J. (1979) *System of Multi-cultural and Pluralistic Assessments: Conceptual and Technical Manual*. Riverside, CA: Institute for Pluralistic Assessment Research and Training.

Mittler, P. (1987) '"Parents are welcome in my school at any time": rhetoric or reality?' in Cross, D. (ed.) *Models of Co-operation in Special Education* (Proceedings of the 10th National Conference of the Australian Association of Special Education, Launceston, Tasmania.

Mittler, P. and Mittler, H. (1982) *Partnership with Parents*. Stratford-on-Avon: National Council for Special Education.

Mortimore, J. and Mortimore, P. (1984) Parents and school. *Education*, 5th October.

Moses, D. (1987) 'The Special Needs Action Programme in Coventry' in D. Moses and S. Hegarty (eds) (1987).

Moses, D., Hegarty, S. and Jowett, S. (1988) *Supporting Ordinary Schools*. Windsor: NFER-Nelson.

Muncey, J. and Ainscow, M. (1983) Launching SNAP in Coventry. *Special Education: Forward Trends* (10) **3**, pp. 8–12.

Newell, P. (1983) *ACE Special Education Handbook: The New Law on Children with Special Needs*. London: Advisory Centre for Education.

Open University (1985) *Special Needs in Education: Guide to the Course*. Milton Keynes: Open University.

Parker, G. (1984) *Into Work: A Review of the Literature about Disabled Young Adults' Preparation for and Movement within Employment*. University of York: Social Policy Unit.

Peters, R. (ed.) (1973) *The Philosophy of Education*. London: Oxford University Press.

Plowden Report. See DES (1967).

Robson, C. (1984) A modular in-service advanced qualification for teachers. *British Journal of In-service Education* (11) **1**, pp. 32–36.

Robson, C., Sebba, J., Mittler, P. and Davies, L. (1987) *Inservice Training and Special Educational Needs: Running Short School-Focussed Courses*. Manchester: Manchester University Press.

Rogers, R. (1986a) *Caught in the Act*. London: CSIE.

Rogers, R. (1985b) *Guiding the Professionals*. London: CSIE.

Rutherford, B. (1986) 'Two and a half years of recording – a schizophrenic response' in J. Wilkinson, *Warnock Seven Years On: A Scottish Perspective*. Glasgow: National Children's Bureau.

Rutter, M., Maughan, B., Mortimore, P. and Ouston, J. (1979) *15 000 Hours*. London: Open Books.

Sandow, S. and Stafford, P. (1986) Parental perceptions and the 1981 Education Act. *British Journal of Special Education* (13) **1**, pp. 19–21.

194   *Meeting Special Needs in Ordinary Schools*

Sayer, J. (1985) 'A whole-school approach to meeting all needs' in J. Sayer and N. Jones (eds) *Teacher Training and Special Educational Needs*. London: Croom Helm.

Sayer, J. (1987) *Secondary Schools for All? Strategies for Special Needs*. London: Cassell.

Sayer, J. and Jones, N. (eds) (1985) *Teacher Training and Special Educational Needs*. London: Croom Helm.

Scottish Education Department (1978) *The Education of Pupils with Learning Difficulties*. HMI, Scotland.

Seligman, M. (1979) *Strategies for Helping Parents of Exceptional Children*. New York: Collier Macmillan.

Special Education: Forward Trends (1983). (10) **4**.

Smith, C. (1983) 'Special Education Aspects of Postgraduate Certificate of Education Courses.' Unpublished report: Department of Special Education, University of Birmingham.

Smith, C. (ed.) (1985) *New Directions in Remedial Education*. Brighton: Falmer Press.

Stillman, A. and Grant, M. (1987) 'The challenge of change: structures, policies and working practices in LEA advisory services' in NFER *Annual Conference Proceedings*. Slough: National Foundation for Educational Research.

Summerfield Report. See DES (1968).

Taylor Report. See DES (1977).

Thomas, D. and Smith, C. (1985) 'Special Educational Needs and Initial Training' in C. Smith (ed.) *New Directions in Remedial Education*. Brighton: Falmer Press.

Thompson, G., Budge, A., Buultjens, M. and Lee, M. (1986) Scotland and the 1981 Education Act. *British Journal of Special Education* (13) **3**, pp. 115–118.

Topping, K. and Wolfendale, S. (eds) (1985) *Parental Involvement in Children's Reading*. London: Croom Helm.

Vernon Report. See DES (1972).

Warnock Report. See DES (1978).

Webster, A. and McConnell, C. (1987) *Children with Speech and Language Difficulties*. London: Cassell.

Wedell, K. and Lambourne, R. (1980) *Psychological Services for Children in England and Wales*. Leicester: British Psychological Society.

Weston, P. (1986) If success had many faces. *Forum* (28) **3**, pp. 79–81.

Widlake, P. (1986) *Reducing Educational Disadvantage*. Milton Keynes: Open University Press.

Wilkinson, J. with Murray, K. (1986) *Warnock Seven Years On: A Scottish Perspective*. Glasgow: National Children's Bureau.

Wolfendale, S. (1983) *Parental Participation in Children's Development and Education*. London: Gordon & Breach.

Wolfendale, S. (1987) *Primary Schools and Special Needs: Policy, Planning and Provision*. London: Cassell.

Wright, H. and Payne, T. (1979) *An Evaluation of a School Psychological Service*. Hampshire Education Department.

Name Index

Subject Index